CONTENTS

Scheldt shipping 1945 *Florent van Otterdyk* 66
Irish Bay Lines – towards a history
   Ian Wilson 79
Sources and acknowledgements 82
Cuban Shipping *Malcolm Cranfield* 83
Messageries Maritime and their post-war
   rebuilding programme.
    Part 2 *Dr Jean-Pierre Burel* 95
SD14 update 2014 *Simon Smith* 103
Ships' brochures: Swedish A class reefers
   1964-1965 *Tony Breach* 110
Putting the Record straight 118
Record review 126
Bosun's Locker 127

Ships in Focus Publications

Correspondence and editorial:
Roy Fenton
18 Durrington Avenue
London SW20 8NT
020 8879 3527
record@rfenton.co.uk

Orders and photographic:
John & Marion Clarkson
18 Franklands, Longton
Preston PR4 5PD
01772 612855
shipsinfocus@btinternet.com

Printed by Amadeus Press Ltd.,
Cleckheaton, Yorkshire.
Designed by Hugh Smallwood, John Clarkson
and Roy Fenton.

SHIPS IN FOCUS RECORD
ISBN 978-0-9928263-1-4

SUBSCRIPTION RATES FOR RECORD

Readers can start their subscription with any
issue, and are welcome to backdate it to receive
previous issues.

	3 issues	4 issues
UK	£27	£35
Europe (airmail)	£29	£38
Rest of the world (surface mail)	£29	£38
Rest of the world (airmail)	£35	£46

SHIPS IN FOCUS

July 201

Before deciding to begin book review, carefully. Being publishers and booksellers ourselves means that we can, we believe, offer readers an informed opinion about what can and should be achieved with a book. But we are also aware that we should not be seen to too readily rubbish other people's books in order to put ours in a good light.

We wanted to shun the approach of those editors who believe that all books range between good and wonderful, and who never again approach a reviewer who is critical about some aspect of a work. In hand with them went reviewers who knew so little of the subject that they were unable to evaluate a book's merit or, especially, whether it made a real contribution in its field. But equally we wanted to avoid being seen as the po-faced, pit-bull reviewer who seizes on a mistake, or – shock horror – a word or phrase he does not personally like, and worries it so much that the reader is left with the impression that the whole book is a dud.

We asked ourselves, just what was the reason for writing and publishing book reviews? Naturally, a review's first purpose is to guide the potential reader as to whether a book is worth buying, and especially whether it offers anything new, and can be relied upon factually. The review also serves the publisher as few if any in a narrow field like shipping history can afford much in the way of publicity, so reviews are a vital part of their promotional effort. Lastly, a review should aim to suggest ways to improve the breed, so that authors and publishers get some constructive feedback on what could be done better, and so that readers have their expectations heightened.

Given the amount of information packed into the kind of shipping book we review, it is most unlikely that every error can be avoided, especially as even the best sources (not least register books, and even registration papers) themselves contain mistakes. Ships in Focus editors (and their long-suffering readers) are also painfully aware of how even multiple proof readings can fail to detect the occasional typographical error. Hence the reviewer has a duty to be fair-minded and – above all – reasonable in his criticisms.

As publishers, we have to accept criticism as well as hand it out. Hence we continue to send our own books for scrutiny to relevant journals. Any other policy would be cowardly.

John Clarkson   Roy Fenton

Messageries Maritimes' *Var*, photographed in the Red Sea during February 1967. See page 95 onwards. *[Charles Protat]*

SCHELDT SHIPPING 1945
Florent van Otterdyk

The liberation of the River Scheldt

Twice in barely thirty years the north western part of Belgium has been involved in severe battles in which tens of thousands of soldiers were killed or severely injured. The year 1914 saw the start of the atrocious trench warfare in 'Flanders' fields' which lasted four years. In 1944 it was the liberation of the River Scheldt and its vital port of Antwerp which resulted in huge casualties amongst the troops involved.

It took just three months to cover the approximately 550 kilometers between the landing beaches in Normandy and the port of Antwerp in the north of Belgium. Once the key had been found in mid-August to unlock Allied troops from the densely wooded 'bocages' of Normandy, the advance of the army was fast. Even the liberation of Paris, originally not part of the Allied plans but executed at the firm demand of the Free French leader Charles de Gaulle, did little to slow the speed with which the Allied forces pursued the enemy. On 25th August 1944 General Dietrich von Choltitz, disobeying a direct order from Hitler, handed over the undamaged capital of France to the French General Leclerc.

On 4th September 1944, barely ten days later, the first British troops set foot in the centre of Antwerp, to the complete surprise of the German military stationed there. It took a few more days to secure the surrounding region and the port.

The vital port which General Eisenhower, Commander-in-Chief of the Allied forces in Europe, desperately wanted, was captured with only minor damage. This result was achieved partly thanks to the efforts of the Belgian resistance. Even before the arrival of Allied troops they had started to sabotage vital industries, halting the production of basic materials needed by the German engineering troops to destroy quays, locks and bridges. The resistance also blew up railway lines and trains, preventing the arrival of German supplies.

But whereas Antwerp and its direct hinterland were liberated by mid-September, the River Scheldt was not. German troops had been able to flee to the northern banks of the river and controlled its access from their strong positions in Zealand.

The reason that no direct action was taken to enable access to the port of Antwerp in September was Field Marshall Montgomery's attempt to cross the Rhine at Arnhem. This made it impossible to deploy the full weight of the army group to clear the river before mid- October, when it took another three weeks of heavy, murderous fighting. After intensive fighting resulting in some 60,000 casualties the German resistance was at last broken on 8th November. The rest of the month of November was needed to clear the river of mines, a threat which continued for months as until the beginning of January German aircraft regularly dropped fresh ones.

At the end of November the vital port of Antwerp could at last be opened for traffic. The first vessel to arrive was listed as the British-flagged steamer *Bertha* (of which no further information can be found) on 25th November, followed a day later by the salvage

tug *Salveda* and a convoy of three small cargo ships, the Norwegian *Lysland* and the Danish *Thyra* and *Fano*. On 28th November military and civilian dignitaries, amongst whom numbered the municipality of the city, were witness to the first large convoy which moored to the sound of a military brass band. It was these ships which are officially recorded as the 'first' arrivals at the liberated port.

As well as clearing of mines in the river, minesweepers based originally in British ports, later in Ostend, had already been busy providing safe navigation channels off the Belgian coast and in the approaches to the river. Similarly with pilotage, Captain Thomas Cowley of the Royal Navy had been called on to set up an international pilot service in which, for the first time, Belgian and Dutch pilots worked together.

Once traffic had resumed it grew very fast, with between 20,000 and 25,000 tons of cargo arriving daily, divided roughly 60% for U.S. and 40% for British troops. To optimize distribution to these armies the port of Antwerp was divided into U.S. and British sectors.

This intense traffic was maintained under all circumstances. In addition to the threat from mines – which did have victims – Germany also used small patrol vessels and even mini-submarines to try to interrupt the flow of ships. The danger of a ship sinking in the navigation channel was always present.

In addition, until the middle of March 1945, the port was constantly fired upon by V-1s and V-2s. More of these missiles hit the Antwerp region than, for instance, harmed London. The V-1s and V-2s were launched from mobile platforms both in Germany and in Holland. Although they did not deter the dock workers from continuing the handling of cargo, the danger meant that a number of vessels loaded with ammunition were directed to Ghent.

Gradually the situation improved, especially after the victory in Europe in early May 1945. In July 1945 the port of Antwerp was considered safe enough to host the U.S. cruiser *Augusta* in which President Harry Truman and his staff crossed the Atlantic to attend the Potsdam Conference. In Antwerp the delegation he headed was met by the principal military and civilian authorities, including General Eisenhower.

Thanks to the fact that the port was able to shorten the logistic chain by some 600 kilometres, the distance between the artificial Mulberry port in Normandy and the fighting Allied forces, it made an important contribution to the war effort.

The photographs illustrating this article were taken by Godfried Van Mullem, a keen ship photographer and contributor to maritime magazines. This collection of negatives and the copyright was bought by the author following the death of the photographer.

For a number of reasons, the pictures date from the second half of 1945. Films were hard to come by and photography by civilians was still censored. In addition, with all the rebuilding to be done in the austere environment immediately post-war, photographing ships was not considered a priority.

ABA (opposite page, top)
Seen outward bound on Sunday 7th October 1945 the *Aba* had, the previous day, landed 465 sick passengers whom she had taken on board in the ports of Boma, Ango-Ango and Matadi of the then Belgian Congo during the first half of September. Only the cross in the funnel pointed to her role as a hospital ship.

The *Aba* had been ordered by the Russian government from Barclay, Curle and Co. at Glasgow, but construction was suspended when

the revolution took place in 1917. Purchased by the Glen Line the 7,347 gross ton vessel was completed as the *Glenapp* in September 1918. Acquired by the British and African Steam Navigation Co. Ltd. two years later she was rebuilt into a passenger ship and returned to service as *Aba* in November 1921.

In December 1929 she had to be towed into Queenstown after her steering gear was severely damaged in a storm. Laid up at the beginning of the thirties she resumed service in 1933

on transfer to Elder Dempster. At the beginning of the Second World War she was requisitioned by the Admiralty and converted into a hospital ship, a role she kept until 1947.

That year she was sold to the Bawtry Steamship Co. Ltd. and renamed *Matrona*. However, upon the removal of the pig iron ballast she capsized in Birkenhead and upon salvage was sold for scrap to T.W. Ward Ltd. who broke her up in their yard at Barrow-in-Furness. A photograph of the capsized *Matrona* appeared on page 150 in 'Record' 3.

ALNWICK

After a career of 32 years the 508 gross ton *Alnwick*, named after the residence of the Duke of Northumberland, was scrapped at Boom, Belgium. The motor coaster was delivered by Hawthorn, Leslie and Co. Ltd. at Hebburn to the Tyne-Tees Shipping Co. Ltd. of Newcastle in May 1936. Coast Lines gained possession of the vessel when they took over Tyne-Tees in 1943, but because of wartime regulations the vessel could not be renamed *Cyprian Coast* until 1946. Nine years later, on 23rd December 1955, she was sunk in a collision but was raised and repaired, giving her another 13 years of trading.

BRITISH COAST

The 888 gross ton *British Coast* was the first of a series of four vessels built by Henry Robb Ltd. at Leith. Although she could be mistaken for a classic dry cargo coaster, the 1933-built vessel actually operated for almost 30 years – apart from the war years – on Coast Lines' regular service between Liverpool and London.

 Requisitioned by the Admiralty in October 1939 she not only operated around the British coasts, but also in West African waters. She was part of the Normandy invasion fleet, transporting cased petrol to the U.S. Army beaches of Omaha and Utah. Surviving the war with no major mishap, she was returned to Coast Lines for whom she operated until sold to Canada in 1964. As *Newfoundland Coast* she served her new owners for 17 more years.

 On 14th July 1981 she was wrecked 16 miles west of Provindenciales, Turks and Caicos Islands.

BOHUS

Ship owners of Sweden had financial reserves which allowed them to put newbuildings into service during the war as even their neutral status did not prevent the loss of a large number of Swedish ships during hostilities. The motor ship *Bohus* is a case in point. Delivered in 1941 by Eriksbergs Mekaniska Verkstad of Göteborg, the 1,250 gross ton vessel was laid up until September 1944, as was the sister *Ahus*, by their owner Trelleborgs Ångfartygs Nya Ab.

In contrast to the dull grey of the majority of the ships sailing at this time, both the Swedish vessels had an attractive, bright appearance in peacetime company colours.

Both motor ships were sold to the Svenska Lloyd of Gothenburg in 1960, and upon transfer in October the *Bohus* became the *Gothia*, remaining under the Swedish flag. That changed in 1963 when she became the Italian *Miseno* for ten years. Sold within Italy she was renamed *Emma D.P.*, an identity she kept for three years, until her transfer to the Cyprus flag as *Glory II*. Under this name she was abandoned by her crew off the southern coast of Turkey in position 36.03 north, 29.31 east on 10th February 1978 when fire broke out in a cargo of timber. The wreck was later towed to Kekova Island where it was left to its fate.

BOSCHFONTEIN

This vessel had the distinction of being converted on several occasions. She was delivered in October 1928 as a 6,280 gross ton cargo steamer by the shipyard of Piet Smit Junior at Rotterdam as the *Nieuwkerk* to the Vereenigde Nederlandsche Scheepvaart Maatschappij for their service to East Africa. She underwent the first major conversion, to a passenger ship, in 1934, the rebuild involving lengthening by about 20 metres, the fitting of a Maier-type bow, and conversion from steam to motor propulsion. It took the shipyard De Schelde of Flushing five and a half months to complete the contract. Renamed *Boschfontein* and now with accommodation for 88 passengers in first class, she operated a round-Africa service, out via East Africa and return via West Africa, and from 1938 on a route from Europe to South Africa.

When the war broke out in Europe, the *Boschfontein* was directed to Pacific services out of Indonesia. This lasted until the spring of 1942 when she became available for the United States war effort. The first voyages for the War Shipping Administration were made as a cargo ship but in September 1942 she was converted into a troop transport. She ran mostly out of San Francisco, and in 1945 was busy trooping to the Pacific islands on which there was fighting with the Japanese. In August she left the Pacific and made one trip to Europe arriving in Antwerp on the 6th October 1945.

On 15th January 1946 she was released by the WSA. The Dutch Government intended to use her as a transport between the Netherlands and the Dutch East Indies but a fire aboard when she was being prepared at the Amsterdamsche Droogdok Maatschappij in September 1946 put an end to this project. Redelivered to VNS, the *Boschfontein* again became a mixed cargo-passenger vessel with accommodation for 79 first class and a number of tourist class passengers, resuming service in May 1947.

She suffered heavy damage in a collision with the Norwegian cargo vessel *Anatina* (4,986/1939) in the vicinity of Sandettie Light Vessel on 16th February 1956 and, in view of the increasing competition from air transport, the passenger accommodation was reduced to 12 and she was renamed *Boschkerk*.

This did not last long as on 19th October 1958, on the eve of a voyage, she was severely damaged by fire in Rotterdam. She was not considered worth repairing, and declared a constructive total loss. Two days before Christmas 1958 a German tug left the Dutch port with the *Boschkerk* in tow for a Hamburg scrap yard.

BULKCRUDE

Ludwig vessels are not known for their beauty. The *Bulkcrude* is typical.

She is one of a little-known standard type ordered by the United States Maritime Commission. The 18,320 deadweight tanker is one of five T3-BF1 types built at Ludwig's own yard which he set up at Norfolk,

Virginia during the early war years under the name Welding Shipyards Inc. These fully welded steam tankers, all completed within an eight-month period, had an overall length of 516 feet and a beam of 70 feet. They can easily be recognized as they have a characteristic poop deck extending half the length of the hull.

The *Bulkcrude* was the fourth of the series, built as yard number 16 and delivered in April 1944. She remained in the Daniel K. Ludwig fleet for 18 years, then being sold to the Greek tycoon Kulukundis in 1962. Renamed *Blue Point* her remaining active life was short as just a year later she went to a Hong Kong scrap yard.

CHANT 26

Nine of the 22 Chant type hulls built by Goole Shipbuilding Co. Ltd. were completed as tankers as this type of ship was originally designed. The thirteen others were completed as dry cargo versions, the Empire F class.

The components for these vessels were manufactured at various works across the United Kingdom and the sections delivered to the different assembly yards, many of them in the Humber area. The Chants were double hulled and, departing from the naming policy used during the war, did not have *Empire* names, but were named *Chant* followed by a number. The dry cargo version did have a name with the prefix *Empire* followed by a name beginning F.

The *Chant 26*, photographed outward bound from Antwerp on 21st July 1945, still has her full defensive weaponry mounted amidships and above the accommodation. A year later the vessel was flying the flag of Finland renamed *T.1* by Finska Angfartygs. Five years later started the 12-year Swedish phase of her

career, being named successively *BT IX*, *Svartskar* and *BT IX*.

Sold in 1963 to Italy, the vessel was owned from then on by various owners under the name *Foca*. In October 1974 the former Channel Tanker was scrapped at La Spezia, one of the few such units still in service at that time.

CHARLES TREADWELL

The Joseph Constantine Steam Ship Line Ltd. of Middlesbrough was the manager of the *Charles Treadwell* until 1950 when this 1,814 gross ton vessel was sold as the *Dundrum Bay* to the Belfast ship owner Lenaghan (see page 80 in this issue). Before she was wrecked on 29th September 1964 the vessel had three more names and two more flags, becoming the *Esito* in 1952 and *Sandra* in 1953, both for Panamanian companies, and *West Indies* under the Liberian flag in 1954.

The *Charles Treadwell* belonged to a standard type known under the administrative name of N3-S-A1, but popularly referred to as 'Jeeps'. A total of 109 units of the 126 initially ordered were built in the USA. There were three variations of the type: the S-A1s, being coal-fired steamers at the special request of Great Britain who took delivery on a lend-lease basis of 36 of these vessels; 59 oil-fired S-A2s; and 14 M-A1 diesel-engined units. With slight variations between the different subtypes their general characteristics were a length of 258.8 feet, a width of 42.1 feet, 2,905 tons deadweight with a speed of 10.5 knots.

The *Charles Treadwell* was a product of the Californian shipyard Pacific Bridge Co. and was delivered to the Ministry of War Transport (post-war the Ministry of Transport) via the United States Maritime Commission - War Shipping Administration who ordered the ship.

FORT SPOKANE

Captain R. Crawford was the happy winner of the coveted gold-headed cane in 1946 as the *Fort Spokane* he commanded was the first of the year to arrive in the port of Montreal on 12th April.

Delivered in June 1943 by the Burrard Dry Dock Co. Ltd. at Vancouver she was, as the name implies, one of the numerous standard ships which were built in Canadian yards for the British Ministry of War Transport.

The name of *Fort Spokane* was only bestowed on the 7,128 gross ton cargo ship in 1944, she being launched as *Fort Norway* but completed as *Mohawk Park*.

These changes of name were probably due to the 'Forts' being transferred to the British Government whereas the identical 'Parks' were operated for the Canadian Government by the Park Steamship Co. Ltd. The latter was formed in 1942 and at its peak controlled 176 vessels, all named after Canadian parks and pleasure gardens.

During the war *Fort Spokane* was managed by Watts, Watts and Co., but was later transferred to Cunard. After her sale in 1951 she remained under the British flag for one more year as *La Orilla* of Buries Markes. The remainder of her career between 1952 and 1964 was spent under the Italian flag under the name *Ariella* owned by Fratelli d'Amico, until scrapped at Trieste.

FRYKEN

Like most vessels of neutral countries, the *Fryken* of the Swedish Ferm Steamship Company, part of the mighty Broström group, was in commercial colours as soon as she resumed trading after the end of the hostilities in Europe.

The 1938-built, 1,024 gross ton vessel had been laid up in Stockholm from 1941 to 1945 as it became too dangerous to operate her in the North Sea, the Baltic and Lake Väner. The only clue that the photograph was taken in 1945 are the liferafts on both sides of the stanchion near the second mast.

Fryken had been ordered from Aalborg Vaerft in Denmark with the specification that she should have the maximum dimensions and load capacity for traversing the Gota Canal all year round. For the efficient handling of cargo there were six derricks each of five tons capacity serving three hatches.

In 1961 she was sold as the *Svano* to Finnish owners. Ten years later she was renamed *Isvania* and spent the last 15 of her active years under the Panamanian flag.

After a brief period of lay-up in Copenhagen the coaster reverted to her original name when she became one of the first acquisitions of the Gothenburg Maritime Centre Foundation. She can still be visited at the Packhuskajen close to the centre of Gothenburg as one of 19 vessels exhibited there.

GEDDINGTON COURT

After a career of 43 years the former *Geddington Court*, second of this name in the Court Line fleet, was broken up in Kaohsiung in December 1971. She was by then a fish factory ship under Japanese flag.

The 6,903 gross ton steamer had been built as yard number 405 by the Northumberland Shipbuilding Co. (1927) Ltd. for the then United British Steam Ship Co. Ltd., which was restyled Court Line Ltd. in 1936. She was a typical tramp of the time, propelled by a triple-expansion steam engine giving her a speed of 10.5 knots.

Very active during the war she survived hostilities without mishap, except for the slight damage probably received during an air attack in early April 1941. In 1951 she was sold to Japan, where owners were little by little rebuilding the depleted merchant fleet, and renamed *Kyoho Maru*, a name kept until broken up. In 1957 she was motorized and four years later converted into a fish factory ship as mentioned above.

GLAUCUS

After 34 years under one name and one owner, the *Glaucus* of the Ocean Steam Ship Co. Ltd. arrived late in October 1955 at Milford Haven to be scrapped by T.W. Ward Ltd.

The 7,582 gross ton ship was one of the first to be ordered by the Liverpool-based Alfred Holt organisation to rebuild and modernize a fleet which had suffered badly during the First World War. *Glaucus*, third of the name in the fleet, was a product of R. and W. Hawthorn, Leslie and Co. Ltd. Launched from their yard in Hebburn on 9th December 1920, the 14-knot vessel was handed over in July of the following year. She had the misfortune on her maiden voyage to go aground in the Yangtse estuary and had to call for the help of tugs. She was one of six Holt-vessels taking part in Operation Husky, but in May 1943 was involved in a collision with the Shell tanker *Macuba* (8,249/1931). In another collision in August 1945 off Holyhead there was such damage that the other vessel involved, the coaster *Blush Rose* (645/1913), sank.

The *Glaucus* was also used for two voyages to bring back Dutch troops to the Netherlands from Indonesia.

IVAN TOPIC

Shortly after being acquired by Slobodna Plovidba Topic at Susak the *Ivan Topic* was in the news as being only the second Jugoslavian vessel to visit Australian ports, when she discharged a full cargo of sulphur from Ancona at Fremantle, Port Lincoln and Geelong.

Until her sale to Ante Topic in 1937, the 4,043 gross ton steamer was in service with the London-based Bowring Steam Ship Co. Ltd. under the name *Ronda*, as which she was built in 1920 by J. Readhead and Sons, South Shields. Ante Topic was a big fan of British vessels, especially those of Hains, from whom he bought several.

The *Ivan Topic* came out of the war unharmed, although she had close encounters such as in April 1943 when the vessel next to her was one of 13 sunk in convoy ONS.5.

In 1946 her name was changed into *Kragujevac*, remaining thus until she was scrapped in 1960, although under different Jugoslav ownership.

KATWIJK

Some vessels have an uneventful career and pass through history almost unnoticed. That summarizes the 33-year life of the 1,589 gross ton *Katwijk*. She was ordered by Wijsmuller of 's Gravenhage, but she was bought on the stocks by Erhardt & Dekkers to whom she was delivered by Jonker & Stans of Hendrik-Ido-Ambacht in February 1921. She was propelled by a triple expansion steam engine of 850 IHP which gave her a nominal speed of 9 knots. Apart from the information that she was transferred within the group to the Wijklijn in 1930 nothing untoward is recorded. That changed at the war's eve. Three weeks before the Netherlands was attacked by Germany the *Katwijk* left Rotterdam for Philadelphia. She was

put at the disposal of the British, was drawn into the Dunkirk evacuation and made numerous voyages in Allied service, some to the despair of convoy commanders as she tended to be too slow to maintain the speed of the convoy. Nevertheless, *Katwijk* was the only vessel in the fleet that reached her Dutch home port unscathed after the war.

She continued to be operated by the Dutch company until sold in 1952. Bought by R. Lunqvist she was put under the Swedish flag as *Etna*, but was lost on 19th January 1954 when she stranded on Scalpay in the Hebrides whilst on a voyage from Garston to Copenhagen.

LACHINEDOC

One of the strange vessels seen on the River Scheldt after its opening for traffic was the 1927-built Laker *Lachinedoc*. She was built for navigation on the Great Lakes and the Welland Canal, hence the main dimensions of 252.5 feet long by 43.3 feet wide and 17.6 feet deep. There were seven holds between the bridge superstructure at the bow and the

accommodation at the stern, over which towered a tall funnel.

She was part of a series of five vessels, her sisters being the *Hamildoc*, *Wellandoc*, *Kingdoc* and *Torondoc* with the suffix –doc standing for 'Dominion of Canada'. Delivered by Swan, Hunter and Wigham Richardson Ltd., she traded for Paterson Steamship Ltd. Towards the end of October 1932 she was involved

in a serious collision with the *John Irwin* (1,926/1929).

In 1942 *Lachinedoc* was put under the Panamanian flag when apparently sold to the United States War Shipping Administration, but she became British-flagged again when controlled by the Ministry of War Transport, managed by Witherington and Everett of Newcastle but registered in London. Laid up in the James River, the *Lachinedoc* was put under the United States flag again. Sold to a subsidiary of the Misener group in 1946 she was refurbished in Canada before resuming service as *Queenston*.

Early in 1961 she became the *Boblodock* after being acquired by the Bob-Lo Ferry Company which stripped her of her superstructure and used her as a passenger pier at Bois Blanc Island, on which island there was then an amusement park. Her remains still seem to be there.

LINCOLN SALVOR

To increase salvage capacity and to establish new salvage centres outside the U.K. vessels of this type were ordered in the USA under the Lend-Lease agreement. However, only four of the six planned to be transferred were in fact delivered to the U.K. The vessels had a length of 183.3, a beam of 37.0 and a draft of 14.8 feet, with a displacement of 1,123 tons. They were equipped with defensive armament, namely a three-inch gun and two 20 mm cannon.

The ships were awarded a standard U.S. nomenclature – ARS – to which a B was added for the vessels to be transferred to Great Britain. As such the *Lincoln Salvor* was laid down by Bellingham Marine Railways and Boatbuilding as the *BARS 9*. Although launched in November 1942 she was only assigned to the United Kingdom on 2nd November 1943 and renamed *Lincoln Salvor* three days later. Once in European waters she served as a coastal salvage vessel.

At the end of 1946 she was returned to the U.S. Navy, but remained in Europe being sold, together with two other BARS, to Greece where she became the *Agerochos* until scrapped in 1964. One of her sisters, *Boston Salvor* (ex *BARS 6*), was struck by a V2 missile at Antwerp on 16th March 1945.

LST 363

A couple of hours after the President of the United States, Harry S. Truman, and his party arrived in Antwerp aboard the cruiser USS *Augusta* (CA 31) en route to the conference at Potsdam, this Landing Ship Tank was spotted in the river.

LST 363 was one of the 1,051 such vessels built to carry troops and supplies to Allied armies fighting in Europe and the Pacific. But long after the hostilities ended, they continued to transport military goods.

LST 363 was built in 1942 by the Bethlehem Steel Company of Quincy, Massachusetts, but was

immediately transferred to the U.K. under the terms of the Lend-Lease Act of 30th November 1942 and commissioned in the Royal Navy on the same day. Two months later she sailed for the Mediterranean and participated in all major campaigns, before being assigned for the Normandy landings. Later she operated for a couple of months on shuttle services between Tilbury, Ostend and Antwerp. Within a month of returning to the USA the landing ship was sold for scrap in December 1947 to a shipbreaker in Norfolk.

NACHMAN SYRKIN

Just a couple of weeks after the armistice had been signed in Reims the *Nachman Syrkin* was spotted on the River Scheldt. The vessel was brand new as it had only been launched at the end of December 1944 by the Delta Ship Building Company at New Orleans, named by the daughter Marie of the person whose name she bore. This was chosen by the Jewish National Workers' Alliance which had raised over two million dollars in War Bonds entitling

them to suggest a name for a Liberty ship.

As can be seen the vessel is still fully equipped with the defensive armament consisting amongst others of a three-inch bow gun, a four- or five-inch stern gun and six 20mm cannon on the bridge aisles and on each side of the fore and mizzen mast.

At first the vessel was managed by Norton Lilly Management for the War Shipping Administration, but later W.R. Rountree and Co. took over this task until she was laid up in 1949.

Bought by Orion Shipping and Trading Co. Inc. of New York the vessel was re-activated two years later as *Seamystery* under the U.S. flag. This did not last long for in 1953 the owners transferred her to one of their subsidiaries under the Panamanian flag. In 1959 she took her last name, *Theomana*, when bought by Spiros Polemis and Sons who continued to operate the vessel under the Panamanian flag until she was scrapped during 1967 in Hong Kong.

OCEAN VULCAN

Completed in February 1942 at Richmond, California by the Todd-California Shipbuilding Division of the Permanente Metals Corporation as one of 30 identical units built in the yard, the *Ocean Vulcan* has the general characteristics of the standard Y-class freighters designed for the British government. Of the same general design as the 'Forts' and the 'Parks' built in Canada, the prefix *Ocean* indicates these vessels (a total of 60 divided between two yards) were United States' constructions.

The cargo ship was fitted with a three-cylinder, triple-expansion reciprocating engine with steam generated by coal-fired boilers. The *Ocean Vulcan* was managed on behalf of the British government by Idwal Williams and Co. with their home port in Cardiff. In 1948 she was acquired by the Lyle Shipping Co. Ltd., Glasgow who renamed her *Cape Nelson*. After 12 years of good service she was sold as *Happy Sunshine*, a name soon changed to *Marine Discoverer*, before being scrapped at Hirao, Japan early in 1967.

PORT SYDNEY

When the Commonwealth and Dominion Line was incorporated in 1914, the 9,136 gross ton *Port Sydney* was one of the five vessels James P. Corry transferred to the new company. At that time the ship was named *Star of England* and had a sister ship, *Star of Victoria*. Propelled by a three-cylinder triple expansion engine of 979 NHP with steam from coal-fired boilers, she had a cruising speed of 13 knots.

Ordered by Corry from Workman, Clark and Co., Belfast she was completed for Commonwealth and Dominion Line. She was in Australian waters when she was requisitioned by the Australian Government as a trooper, receiving the pennant number A15. She was converted at Cockatoo Island Dockyard, Sydney in the summer of 1914 to transport some 524 troops and 511 horses.

When Commonwealth and Dominion Line became part of Cunard the vessels not only got the funnel colours of the new parent company, but were also renamed, the *Star of England* becoming *Port Sydney* in 1916. Decommissioned in November 1917 she reverted to commercial use. Between the two wars she traded between the U.K. and Australasian ports, carrying amongst others material for the Sydney Harbour Bridge.

For most of the years 1939 to 1944 she was trading to the USA but in the latter year, owing to the age of her boilers, she was placed on shorter voyages. After 34 years of loyal services she was sold for scrap in the U.K. arriving at Preston on 19th December 1948. Over the years the vessel steamed 1,670,000 miles burning more than half a million tons of coal.

RADCOMBE
Worn out and in dire need of a thorough overhaul, the 4,753 gross ton *Radcombe* is seen on the River Scheldt loaded down to her marks.

She had been built at the Glen Yard of William Hamilton and Co. Ltd., Port Glasgow in 1927 and delivered as the *Nikola Pasic* to Yugoslav owners in Dubrovnik. Taken over by the Ministry of War Transport in 1941 she was renamed *Radcombe* the same year, with management allocated to P.D. Hendry and Sons of Glasgow but registered in Middlesbrough.

In 1946 the vessel was returned to the Yugoslav flag and as the *Kozara* continued to ply the oceans for another 18 years. Sold for scrap at the end of 1964 she arrived at her final destination, Sveti Kajo, Split in early January 1965.

ROSEMONT
Photographed in August 1945 during her Panamanian interlude as *Rosemont*, this modern looking vessel spent most of her trading career under the Finnish flag.

Delivered in December 1938 to the Suomen Etelä-Amerikan Linja by the Crighton-Vulcan yard at Åbo two years after the building contract was signed, the motor vessel *Aurora* was, together with her sisters *Atlanta* and *Bore X*, with a speed of 15 knots and a large refrigeration capacity, an instant success on the route between Europe and the east coast of South America.

After the virtual closing of the Baltic Sea due to the German occupation of Norway and Denmark, the Finnish trade had to make use of the small port of Petsamon, which is now part of Russia.

In the summer of 1941 the *Aurora* was taken over by the United States government after the vessel had changed course to New York when on a northbound voyage from South America. After extensive repairs had been made to the midships section, which had been badly damaged by fire, she was put into service as *Rosemont* under the Panama flag. In 1946 she was returned to her Finnish owners and given back her original name. The *Aurora* was the first Finnish vessel to be equipped with radar, which she had been given during the war.

In 1954 her original diesel engine was replaced by a new one. She was the oldest vessel in the fleet when sold in 1964 to Greece, under whose flag and the name *Ioannis* she ended her career in 1971, broken up in China.

SAMOS

The larger part of the vessels trading into Antwerp after the hostilities were, as can be easily understood, the various standard ships built during hostilities. Within this category the Liberties formed the large majority. Not only were the EC2s under the U.S. flag common visitors but there were also numerous 'Sams', Liberties transferred to the British flag under the Lend-Lease Act.

As can be seen, it was not a sunny summer day when the *Samos* left the port in ballast, still fully equipped with defensive armament.

The steamer had been built by the Bethlehem Fairfield Shipyard in Baltimore as yard number 2218 and delivered in 1943 as *Tench Tilghman* to the United States Maritime Commission. Bare boat chartered to the Ministry of War Transport she became the *Samos*,

managed by Elder Dempster Lines and registered in London. The shipping company bought the ship outright in 1947 for £135,261, renamed her *Zini* and registered her in Liverpool.

After 12 years of service she was sold out of the fleet. As *San Salvador* she completed another nine years of good service under the Liberian flag. She was scrapped at La Spezia at the end of 1968.

WAR PINDARI

The centrally-placed expansion trunk betrays this vessel as a tanker. The 5,548 gross ton *War Pindari* was one of the Z-type standard tankers specially designed in the First World War for the carriage of heavy fuel oil. Built by Lithgows Ltd. at Port Glasgow she was put under the management of C.T. Bowring and Co. on delivery in March 1920.

The vessel had the basic dimensions of 410 by 52.4 feet of the standard ships Britain had built during the conflict. In contrast to most of the other such ships, the Z-type tankers were oil fired.

A year after her delivery she was transferred to the Admiralty and continued to be operated under her original name as part of the Royal Fleet Auxiliary. Her profile remained almost

unchanged from the basic design, the major alteration being the replacing of the pole mast between the funnel and bridge superstructure with a pair of orthodox masts.

In 1948 the tanker was sold to John Harker Ltd. and renamed *Deepdale H*. Four years later she became the Italian *Carignano*, but not for long as she was scrapped during the winter of 1954 at Blyth.

Top: *Como* of 1910 was bought from Ellerman's Wilson Line by H.P. Lenaghan in September 1945 and sold to Hull owners in February 1946. She ended up under the Turkish flag and was scrapped in 1969. *[J. and M. Clarkson]*

Middle: *Ballyholme Bay* of 1908 at Bristol on 4th December 1949. British-built but German-flagged, she had been taken as a prize at Copenhagen in May 1945. Lenaghan owned her from 1947 to 1950. *[J. and M. Clarkson collection]*

Bottom: The second *Bangor Bay* was built in 1941 at Scotstoun as *Empire Mallory*. Lenaghan bought her as a total loss in 1948 and had her repaired. *[J. and M. Clarkson collection]*

IRISH BAY LINES – TOWARDS A HISTORY

Ian Wilson

Nowadays the movements of ships, the founding and operating of fleets, and the maritime scene at large are rarely reported in the media. But in the 1940s and 1950s local companies and local crews were newsworthy. The giddy rise and abject fall of Irish Bay Lines and its flamboyant principal, Henry P. Lenaghan, were frequently mentioned in the 'Belfast Telegraph' and 'Belfast News Letter'. Weekly updates on their ships' movements were even printed. But apart from the newspapers' files, the facts in 'Lloyd's Register', and a few morsels on the internet, little or nothing has ever been recorded about the firm. Here is a selection of photographs of some of the fleet which, it is hoped, will stimulate interest among readers, who may be able to help with research towards a more detailed fleet list, plus attendant information and anecdotes.

Lenaghan was a mystery man when he came on the shipping scene. Said to originate from Eire, his first recorded ship is the wooden steam coaster *Hill*, bought during the war and wrecked on the County Wicklow coast in 1944. The salvage of the sunken *Kerry Coast* in the Mersey later in 1944 no doubt yielded a good profit, as Lenaghan sold her on to the British and Irish Steam Packet Company. Apparently, his letter to Belfast Harbour Commissioners asking permission to dry dock her came hand-written on everyday notepaper and was refused (the work was done in Dublin). Yet only six years later he had built for his operations a new office block in Belfast's 'sailortown' and was operating passenger and cargo ships, and tugs, world-wide. Where had the profits come from?

The probable answer is the transport of emigrants: Lenaghan's finest ship was the former Norddeutscher Lloyd steamer *Nurnberg* which he acquired in 1948 and sent to Trieste to be converted to carry 1,024 passengers. Units of the Royal Netherlands Army were repatriated on her, and what was no doubt a lucrative charter arranged with the International Refugee Organisation, who are known to have subsidised ship owners who were building or converting ships for their work. A number of voyages were made to Australia and New Zealand

with displaced persons, on one of which Lenaghan, his wife Millicent and two children sailed in staterooms. A Fremantle newspaper covered the story with the headline 'Came in Migrant Ship - His Own!'

Having managed the *Empire Islander* and *Empire Newfoundland* for the Ministry of War Transport, Lenaghan also took on bareboat charter the *Empire Glencoe* which had been launched as *Atlas* at Emden in 1941, but which was bombed and sunk in

Hamburg before completion. She was to be renamed *Bantry Bay* but this never happened, and a blow to operations came in 1954 when Isbrandtsen and Company of New York undertook a legal action claiming breach of the terms of her charter to them by Lenaghan. They had the *Dundalk Bay* arrested and, in 1959, two years after she had been sold, there was still another legal case being fought over the *Dundalk Bay*. These may have contributed to Lenaghan's bankruptcy.

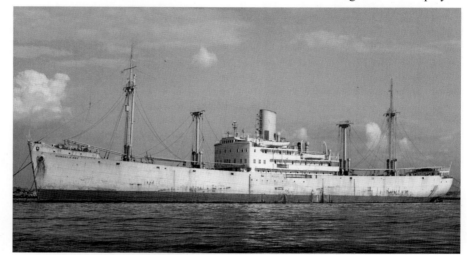

Both these views of the *Dundalk Bay* give the appearance she is laid up. She is depicted at buoys in the view above dated September 1954, and from other photographic evidence was in the same position and condition at least from May to November that year. One of the photographers noted that she had a 'cream-coloured hull', although by now it was becoming rust-streaked. In the photograph below she is in a London dock - perhaps a later view taken when she was under arrest. She was sold in 1957 to a company associated with J.A. Billmeir and renamed *Westbay*. The ship was broken up in 1962, following, it is said, severe engine damage. *[Laurence Dunn; John Anderson]*

Among the other ships to fly Lenaghan's flag (white with a red diamond and the firm and owner's initials) were the *Brown's Bay* and *Dundrum Bay*, both of the U.S. Maritime Commission's standard N3-A1 class, the latter being chartered to the Hall Corporation of Canada Ltd. for the Great Lakes coal trade.

Interestingly, the firm also owned at least seven tugs, no doubt doing good business on the post-war salvage and towing scenes. One, the *Lenamill*, built in 1940 as the *Arngast* for the Kriegsmarine, was proudly billed as the second most powerful tug in the world, and was later bought by Bugsier. In 1949 Lenaghan was reported to be in Singapore where *Lenamill* was to be stationed after she completed towing an Italian warship.

Lenaghan's new-found riches brought him a plush lifestyle including a large yacht and a shiny limousine which featured a drinks cabinet, something to impress the gawping bystanders. His name, however, means very little today. By 1958 a mighty fall was complete: an official liquidator of the firm was appointed and Lenaghan was declared bankrupt. His address was given as Cultra Manor, County Down, a fine Victorian mansion once the home of an eminent diplomat, Sir Robert Kennedy, and now the headquarters of the Ulster Folk and Transport Museum. It is said he bought it with grand designs, but never actually resided there.

To general surprise, however, Lenaghan returned to the shipping scene in 1966, having had his bankruptcy annulled. He formed Irish Tankers Ltd. and bought the *Andrea Brovig*, renamed *Dundrum Bay*, but both this and a further venture in 1973 were little more than fiascos. There are also unconfirmed stories of failed purchase schemes. The latter attempt to reclaim the glory days was with the tanker *British Reliance*, renamed *Bangor Bay* and officially owned by Atlantic Research Ltd., Bermuda, but she made only one or two loaded voyages before being arrested and sold at public auction, just like the *Dundrum Bay*.

'Boom and bust': the cycle of ship owning is certainly exemplified by Henry P. Lenaghan. Let us hope it is possible in time to compile a proper account of Irish Bay Lines.

Empire Glencoe of 1941 was another German prize, taken unfinished as *Atlas* at Kiel in May 1945 and completed in 1948. In 1952 Lenaghan intended to rename her *Bantry Bay*, but this never happened and in 1955 she was sold back to German ownership, surviving until demolished in Spain during 1976. *[World Ship Society Ltd.]*

Dingle Bay (above) had been built as the *New Westminster City* by Gray of West Hartlepool in 1929. Lenaghan bought her in 1948 and sold her to Japan in 1951 to be renamed *Asakaze Maru*. She was scrapped at Sakai in October 1965. She is seen lying at buoys in Fowey on a pleasant summer's day. *[Marion Love/National Maritime Museum]*
Photographed in London on 12th August 1950, the *Dundrum Bay* (below) was built as the *Charles Treadwell* in 1943 at Alameda, California, and spent some time under Lenaghan's ownership trading on the Great Lakes. When she made her first visit to her home port, Belfast, on 7th February 1952, with coal from Hull, the 'Belfast News Letter' deemed it worthy of a photograph; sadly, such once-natural local connection with ships and seafarers is largely a thing of the past almost everywhere. *[G.A. Osbon/World Ship Society Ltd.]*

The hulk of the *Lenaship* near Portaferry, Strangford Lough, County Down, about 1960 (above left). This large tug had been built far away in Olympia, Washington in 1944 as the *Secure*. Lenaghan was her owner by 1954, but sold her to John Lee of Belfast a year or two later. Lee ran a shipbreaking operation which involved demolition of several 'Flower' class corvettes and the *Empire Tana*, one of the ships sunk to form a Mulberry Harbour. Remains of ships are still visible at low tide and divers call the *Empire Tana* 'Lee's wreck'. *[Fred Rainey]*

Bugsier's ocean-going tug *Wotan* (above right) was owned by Irish Bay Lines Ltd. as *Lenamill* between 1947 and 1950. She had been built in 1940 by H.C. Stülcken Sohn, Hamburg for the Kriegsmarine as *Arngast*. *Wotan* was with Bugsier until 1970 when broken up at Bremerhaven. *[J. and M.Clarkson collection]*

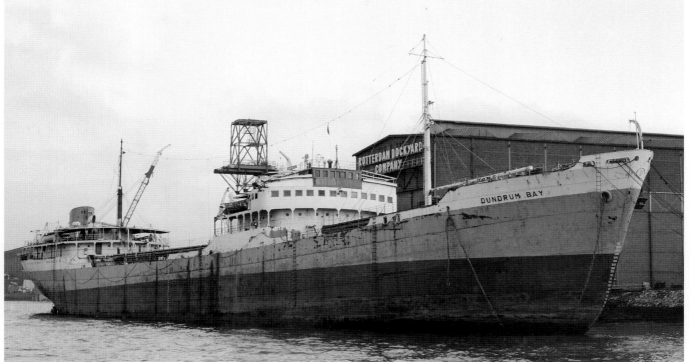

The only ship of the short-lived Irish Tankers Ltd., *Dundrum Bay*, quite possibly after she had been sold to Liberian flag operators at auction in 1968 (above). The photograph is undated but another shot shows she was still berthed in Rotterdam in July 1970. The author can at least claim to have seen one Bay: when on a cruise round Rotterdam docks as a ship-spotting student in 1973, the *Dundrum Bay* was laid up. She had been built by Lithgows of Port Glasgow as the *Andrea Brovig* in 1948 and was scrapped at Bilbao in 1974. *[World Ship Society Ltd.]*

British Reliance of 1950 was the second *Bangor Bay* from 1973 to 1974. She then briefly became the Greek-flagged *Ocean Princess* (above) until she was demolished in Spain during April 1975. *[William Schell]*

Provisional list of ships owned or managed

Irish Bay Lines
HILL (496/1920) 1942-1944
COMO (1,246/1910) 1945-1946
BANGOR BAY (1) (1,407/1919) 1945-1946
BALLYHOLME BAY (1) (1,241/1908) 1947-1951
BANTRY BAY (673/1911) 1947
BANGOR BAY (2) (6,327/1941) 1947-1954
DINGLE BAY (4,995/1929) 1948-1951
EMPIRE GLENCOE (4,854/1948) 1948-1956 (chartered from Ministry of Transport; intended to be renamed BANTRY BAY)
DUNDALK BAY (5,579/1936) 1948-1957
DUNDRUM BAY (1,814/1943) 1950-1952
BROWN'S BAY (1) (1,934/1943) 1950-1953 r/n BALLYHOLME BAY (2) 1952
BROWN'S BAY (2) (1,722/1948) 1953-1955

Managed for Ministry of War Transport
EMPIRE ISLANDER (3,539/1944) 1944-1949 (?)
EMPIRE NEWFOUNDLAND (2,066/1943) 1943-1949 (?)

Irish Tankers Ltd.
DUNDRUM BAY (2) (8,988/1948) 1966-1968

Atlantic Research Ltd., Bermuda (Irish Tankers (Ulster) Ltd., managers)
BANGOR BAY (3) (11,026/1950) 1973

Tugs
LENASHIP (1892)
LENASHIP II
LENABAY
LENADIL
LENASHIP (1944)
LENADEE
LENAMILL (1947-1950)
H.P. LENAGHAN

A last look at *Dundrum Bay* as she departs from Rotterdam on 16th February 1974 in the care of local harbour tugs bound for the breakers. The towing gear of the deep-sea tug, out of view but leading the procession, can be seen above the bow tug. [William A. Schell]

SOURCES AND ACKNOWLEDGEMENTS

SOURCES AND ACKNOWLEDGEMENTS
We thank all who gave permission for their photographs to be used, and for help in finding photographs we are particularly grateful to Tony Smith, Jim McFaul and David Whiteside of the World Ship Photo Library; to Ian Farquhar, F.W. Hawks, Peter Newall, Russell Priest, William Schell; and to David Hodge and Bob Todd of the National Maritime Museum, and other museums and institutions listed.

Research sources have included the Registers of William Schell and Tony Starke, 'Lloyd's Register', 'Lloyd's Confidential Index', 'Lloyd's Shipping Index', 'Lloyd's War Losses', 'Mercantile Navy Lists', 'Marine News', 'Sea Breezes' and 'Shipbuilding and Shipping Record'. Use of the facilities of the World Ship Society, the Guildhall Library, the National Archives and Lloyd's Register of Shipping. Particular thanks also to Heather Fenton for editorial and indexing work, and to Marion Clarkson for accountancy services.

A class reefers
Sources used: 'Lloyds' Registers', 'Lloyd's Confidential Indexes', 'Marine News', Salen Archives at Cool Carriers.

CUBAN SHIPPING
Malcolm Cranfield

The island of Cuba in the West Indies was discovered by Christopher Columbus in 1492. It was soon to become a Spanish colony, ruled by a Spanish governor based in Havana. Following its creation in 1865 Compañía Transatlántica Española (the Spanish Transatlantic Line) carried most of the island's trade. However, from 1877 Ward Line's New York and Cuba Mail Steamship Company, and from 1899 the Munson Steamship Line, took advantage of increased United States' involvement in the Cuban economy.

From 1868, in what became known as the Ten Years' War, Carlos Manuel de Céspedes led the first serious attempt to achieve independence from Spain. Increased tensions between Spain and the United States, which culminated in the Spanish-American War, then led to a Spanish withdrawal in 1898, and by 1902 U.S. companies controlled 80% of Cuba's ore exports and owned most of the sugar and cigarette factories. In presidential elections on 31st December 1901, Tomás Estrada Palma, a United States citizen, became the only candidate when his adversary, General Bartolomé Masó, withdrew in protest against favouritism towards the United States.

The Cuban republic subsequently enjoyed significant economic development but also corruption and despotic leadership, notably by 'Batista' (Fulgencio Batista y Zaldivar) who led the country after a revolution in 1933 until losing power in 1944 elections and seizing it back in a 1952 coup.

Fidel Castro, then a young lawyer and communist politician, with his brother Raúl, resolved to overthrow Batista and on 26th July 1953 led an attack on the Moncada Barracks near Santiago de Cuba. Although the attack ended in failure and imprisonment, the Batista government in 1955 released the brothers who went into exile in Mexico where they met the Argentine revolutionary Ernesto Che Guevara. A landing in Cuba by Castro and Che from Mexico in the yacht *Granma* with 82 crew in December 1956 saw the group fleeing into the Sierra Maestra mountains and beginning a guerrilla campaign aided by Frank Pais.

Batista finally fled on 1st January 1959 and Castro took over, suppressing all opposition and incurring the wrath of the United States government, which imposed a trade embargo on 3rd February 1962, while inviting the Soviet Union to participate in Cuba's business and defence. In the 1961 New Year's Day Parade, the Communist administration exhibited Soviet tanks and other weapons while tensions peaked during the October 1962 Cuban missile crisis. Thereafter life in Cuba became increasingly difficult and many people either left the country or faced imprisonment or execution.

Still today foreign shippers charge a premium for serving Cuba because the United States prohibits ships coming from Cuba to dock at United States ports.

Shipping services

Until 1959 shipping to Cuba had been largely controlled by U.S. and European lines within the liner conference system, allowing little scope for private Cuban shipping companies to flourish. The Cuban section of the Europe-West Indies WITASS (West India Transatlantic Steamship Lines) Conference had included Compañía Transatlántica Española and major lines from Germany, France, Belgium, Holland, Italy, Norway and Sweden plus Pacific Steam Navigation which had acquired John Glynn's share in 1933. The Isbrandsten-controlled Ward Line, purchased in 1955 by Compañía Naviera García and operated as Ward-García Line until 1959, was briefly resurrected in the Communist era as 'Cubamex' (Cuba, Mexico and West Indies Steam Ship Company) but was shunned by the Conference and ceased business in 1962.

Seatrain Lines had meanwhile begun the innovative practice of hauling rail cars by ship from New York to Havana but this service also closed when Castro came to power. This company had started in business in 1928 as the Over-Seas Steam Ship Co. Ltd. of Montreal with the ferry *Seatrain* which was renamed *Seatrain New Orleans* on delivery of two new ships in 1932. At this point the company was renamed Seatrain Lines Inc. and moved to New Orleans. Named *Seatrain New York* and *Seatrain Havana*, the new ships were capable of carrying 100 fully loaded railcars on their four decks.

During the 1950s the main outside opposition to the established lines came from the shipping department of Ferromar (formerly Bemony Trading), managed by Van Meerbeeck of Antwerp, which had in 1957 established a new company in Havana named Naviera Polaris S.A. ('NAVPOL') with the intention of it becoming Cuba's national fleet. In February 1959 NAVPOL had applied to join WITASS with four Cuban-flagged ships, a plan which was soon abandoned when Castro took over the country.

The Spanish domiciled firm of Naviera Herrara, which changed its name in 1916 to Empresa Naviera de Cuba, was the first Cuban line but there were few others until 'Mambisa' was created in 1959 by the new Communist government.

Although in 1948 the U.S. Government gave to Empresa Naviera de Cuba four C1-M-AV1-type ships to service the trade to New York, by 1953 this company was close to bankruptcy and the ships were then chartered to Naviera Vacuba S.A. who by early 1959 had sought to enter the conference of lines operating between UK and Havana via New York. However, these ships, given the names *Bahia de Mariel*, *Bahia de Matanzas*, *Bahia de Nipe* and *Bahia de Nuevitas*, very soon became units of the Mambisa fleet.

An arm of the state bank, Banco Cubano del Comercio Exterior, had in the mid-1950s become increasingly involved in Cuban shipping, sourcing for local firm Naviera Garcia four small new ships from Germany, then facilitating their purchase of Ward Line and in 1957 enticing the Bilbao-based Sr. José de Navas Escuder, together with the sugar traders Czarnikow-Rionda, to create a new Cuban shipping company named Naviera de Navas. Three ships were initially purchased, being *Rio Jibacoa* (ex *Coulbreck*), *Rio Caonao* (ex *Thésée*) and *Rio Damuji* (ex *Uskport*). Four new ships were ordered in 1957 from Atlantic Shipbuilding at Newport, Monmouthshire and delivered between 1958 and 1960 as *Pinar del Rio*, *Las Villas*, *Matanzas* and *Habana*.

Then, in May 1958, the bank purchased eight strikebound ships from Canadian National Steamships which the Seafarers' International Union initially prevented from sailing.

Canadian Cruiser and *Canadian Constructor* became *Manuel Ascunce* and *Conrado Benitez*, joining the Mambisa fleet, while sister ship *Canadian Challenger* remained as the *Ciudad de La Habana* until sold to Hellenic Lines in 1966 and renamed *Italia*. The smaller sisters *Canadian Conqueror*, *Canadian Highlander*, *Canadian Leader*, *Canadian Observer* and *Canadian Victor* never traded and were all broken up in Spain during 1965.

Mambisa

Started in 1959 to operate between Cuba and the United States, Empresa Consolidada de Navegación Mambisa subsequently appointed general agents in Europe (for the U.K., Charles Hill of Bristol) and in December 1960, whilst en route from Hamburg for Cuba, the *Rio Damuji* loaded 80 tons of oil at Liverpool with the chartered German-owned *Indus* following. Within a year Mambisa was providing two or three sailings a month from North Europe to Cuba and operating 19 ships with newbuilds from East Germany (*Sierra Maestra*) and Poland (*Comandante Camilo Cienfuegos*) joining in 1962. There was even talk of Mambisa becoming a 'tolerated outsider' of the Conference but antagonism with the West was increasing and by February 1962 Cuba was sourcing most commodities from the Eastern block. While the Soviet Union had previously provided the majority of the tonnage, in November 1962 Cuba, East Germany, Czechoslovakia and Poland created a joint service named 'CUBALCO (Cuba-Baltic Continent Freight Service) managed from Rostock.

While Mambisa had initially aimed to have one hundred ships in operation by 1965, the fleet grew more slowly than planned, reaching forty ships by 1967 and sixty by 1981. Instead, the Government's chartering arm, Empresa Cubana de Fletes ('CUFLET'), grew in importance while many ships were owned or managed by newly created companies. The relationship between these new companies and Mambisa was often indistinct.

From the early 1970s, presumably seeking to circumvent sanctions imposed on Cuban flagged ships, a policy of flagging out newly purchased ships was implemented with many being registered in Somalia and given names ending *Islands*. Blue Sea Shipping Company was established in Vaduz, Liechtenstein, for that purpose. This policy accelerated in the early 1990s with the creation of a new company named Naviera Poseidon, it seems primarily to allow Cuba to be involved in international trading, and the use of other flags of convenience so by 1998 the original target of one hundred ships was broadly reached.

Other state-owned companies

While several specialist companies were created in 1959 by the Castro government to operate tankers, cement carriers, refrigerated ships, tugs and fishing vessels, over the years several ships were switched between Mambisa and these operators. For example, a new company named Empresa Navegación Caribe (Caribbean Navigation Company) was created in the 1960s to manage ferries and coasters while also given management responsibility for the tanker fleet.

The dissolution of the Soviet Union in 1990 left Cuba in a difficult position as the USSR was its trading partner and backer of its merchant fleet. Cuba's merchant shipping then had to find new ways to survive and continue to serve the island's trade despite the United States embargo. Empresa de Navegación Mambisa and CUFLET were transferred from the Ministry of Transport to the Ministry of Fisheries within a division called Pesport. However, in 1995 the Cuban Government restructured the sector so that the Ministry of Fisheries retained only the fishing-related activities while the shipping activities were transferred to a new body named the Antares Association.

New companies introduced in the 1990s, initially controlled by Pesport, had included the above mentioned Naviera Poseidon with, by 1998, eleven vessels of between 15,000 and 24,000 deadweight tonnes; Friomar Naviera operating nine ships with reefer capability and Naviera Mar. America serving routes in the Caribbean, and to Central and South America. More important was Naviera del Caribe ('Carimar') with ten vessels, five being container ships with a capacity of between 400 and 700 TEUs which linked Cuba with neighbouring hubs, partly in co-operation with foreign partners such as CGM from 1995. Opening services from Italy and Spain, Coral Container Line soon went on to take over Mambisa's cargo liner services from Canada and North Europe with 'Dnepr' class and two Wismar-OBC type ships of 24,000 deadweight tonnes and 863 TEU capacity, named *Santa Rita* and *Santa Rosa*, acquired from the Oetker Group and renamed *Caribbean Queen* and *Caribbean Princess*. However, in 1999 the Cuban-controlled but Dutch-based Melbridge Container Line, created in 1994, took over Coral's services between North Europe and Cuba while the Cuban-owned, Panama-based Melfi Lines, founded in 1981, took over the Canada service in 2003. Meanwhile in 2002, as Cuba started slowly to open its foreign trade, a rival service from Italy and Spain was launched by Costa Container Lines leading to the closure of Coral Container Line.

As the 20th century progressed, Cuba had entered more shipping-related joint ventures with foreign interests. These included, in London in 1973, Anglo-Caribbean Shipping Co. Ltd. to act as brokers and agents for CUFLET, in 1979 Nippon Caribbean Shipping Company based in Tokyo and, in 1991 Nordstrand Maritime and Trading Co. Ltd. based in Piraeus, Greece, which still manages much of the Cuban fleet.

Empresa Cubana de Fletes (CUFLET)

This organisation was created by the Cuban Government to charter ships to serve Cuba, which must have been a difficult task given the sanctions imposed by the United States. While many of the ships were voyage chartered several became regular visitors to Cuba, perhaps as they were then banned from visiting United States ports. These had included *Huntsville*, *Huntsland*, *Avis Faith*, *Ravens* and *Olebratt* and possibly also *Redestos* and *Stanwear*. It is fascinating to note that several ships subsequently owned by Cuba were named after these ships. Other ships, such as *Alitric*, were time chartered and often had the name CUFLET painted on their hulls. It is unfortunate that prostitutes became known as 'Cufletera'.

Cuban shipping today

In September 2013, Shanghai Shipyard Co. Ltd. delivered to Cuba the *Josefa*, the tenth and final bulk carrier of 35,000 deadweight tonnes from an order by Empresa Importadora General del Transporte (EIGT), on behalf of Grupo Acemex, with Chinese state company China National Machinery Import and Export Corporation (CMC) and financed by China's Eximbank. The first ship in the series was the *Abdala*, delivered in August 2011. All ten ships are managed by Nordstrand under the Panama flag.

The author wishes to thank Carlos Vadir Goñiz Fariñas for assistance with the research for this article.

CARIBE

The privately owned Cuban company Naviera Garcia had, in the mid 1950s, purchased the Ward Line, one of whose ships was the *Caribe*, an N3-S-A2 type built at Westwego, New Orleans, in 1945 as *John Leckie*, and acquired by Ward in 1948. Photographed on the Houston Ship Channel, *Caribe* was sold in 1961 to Edmond H.Smith of New Orleans and renamed *Pensacola*. Unfortunately, she sank off Puerto Rico on 15th February 1966 during a voyage from Mobile to Trinidad. *[Malcolm Cranfield collection]*

RIO JIBACOA

Purchased by Naviera de Navas of Havana in 1957 and given the name *Rio Jibacoa*, in 1961 she became a unit of Empresa Consolidada de Navegación Mambisa, the state shipping line created by the new communist government led by Fidel Castro, and was photographed arriving at Montréal in November 1966. Built by Lithgows at Port Glasgow in 1946 for the Dornoch Steam Ship Co. Ltd. (Lambert Brothers, managers) as *Coulbreck*, she was renamed *Dundrennan* in 1954 when Glen and Co. took over management of the Dornoch company, which was sold in 1956 to Harrisons (Clyde) Ltd., a new company formed by Gow, Harrison and Co. *Rio Jibacoa* was broken up in Spain at the end of 1969. *[Harry Stott/Malcolm Cranfield collection]*

RIO CAONAO

Purchased by the Batista-led régime in 1957, *Rio Caonao* was initially registered in the name of the Banco Cubano del Comercio Exterior and transferred to the Oficina de Fomento Maritimo Cubano (Cuban Maritime Development Office) in 1959. In 1961 she became a unit of Empresa Consolidada de Navegación Mambisa, the state shipping company created by the new government, and was photographed arriving at Montréal in September 1966. *Rio Caonao* had been built in 1948 by Davie Shipbuilding at Lauzon in Canada as *Thésée* for Société Navale Caennaise of France and was broken up at Tuxpan, Mexico, in 1975, it is thought after a long period laid up at Havana. *[Harry Stott/Malcolm Cranfield collection]*

LUIS ARCOS BERGNES (above)
Named after a fighter who had died in 1956 resisting the Batista régime, the 16.5-knot reefer *Luis Arcos Bergnes* was purchased by Cuba in 1964. Built in 1950 at Tønsberg, Norway, as *Alvdal* for A/S Moltzau of Oslo, she had traded from 1954 until 1964 as *Frubel Clementina* for Belgian Fruit Lines. Operated by Empresa Cubana de Naviera, she was broken up at San Esteban de Pravia in Spain where she arrived on 6th October 1977. She was a regular caller at Montréal and is seen sailing for Havana in July 1971. *[Marc Piché/Malcolm Cranfield collection]*

LA LIMA (middle)
Seen passing Hoek van Holland, outbound from Rotterdam, on 26th June 1976 is Mambisa's refrigerated cargo ship *La Lima*, coincidentally bound for Elsinore where she had been built in 1959 as *Yugala* for D/S Torm A/S, Copenhagen. Possibly in order to circumvent trade restrictions with Cuba, the ship had in 1966 been purchased by Imextracom Etablissement of Bulgaria, and given the name *Algenib*, prior to transfer to the Cuban Government who initially named the ship *Realengo 18*. As Mambisa's *La Lima* she then sailed from Havana on New Year's Day 1967, subsequently making several voyages to North European ports before being transferred to Empresa Navegación Caribe in 1984, thereafter trading closer to home. *La Lima* arrived at Cartagena, Colombia, on 24th November 1993 to be broken up. *[Malcolm Cranfield collection]*

CONRADO BENITEZ
Named after a teacher who was murdered in 1961 by insurgents opposed to Fidel Castro, the 1947 Canadian-built *Conrado Benitez*, operated from 1962 by Mambisa, was photographed sailing from Antofagasta, Chile. Built as *Canadian Constructor*, she was operated between 1952 and 1958 by Canadian National (West Indies) Steamships Ltd. until acquired by the Cuban government and renamed *Ciudad de Montréal*. Sister ship *Canadian Cruiser* became *Ciudad de Detroit* and then *Manuel Ascunce*. Apparently laid up at Havana from early 1977, *Conrado Benitez* was hulked in 1980 and later sunk as a target off Cuba. *[Daslav Petricio/ Marc Piché collection]*

CARLOS MANUEL DE CESPEDES
The Canadian war-built Fort type *Carlos Manuel de Céspedes*, photographed arriving at Rotterdam in early May 1969 from Mormugao, was operated by Mambisa from 1968 until sold for breaking up at Vinaròs, Spain, where she arrived in July 1977. Built in 1943 as *Fort Moose* and taking the Canadian name of *Haligonian Prince* between 1948 and 1950, she was then operated until 1966 by Counties Ship Management as *Tulse Hill*. Then trading as *Astronaftis*, owned by George Dracopoulos (Empros Lines) of Piraeus, she, along with the same owner's sister ship *Atromitos* and the Liberty type *Zela M.*, was purchased by Cuba in mid 1968. [*Malcolm Cranfield collection*]

CERRO PELADO
One of a series of ten ships built for Cuba by Spanish yards in 1965 and 1966 for operation by Mambisa, *Cerro Pelado* was photographed sailing from Antofagasta, Chile. After arriving at Cienfuegos in June 1986, *Cerro Pelado* was next reported arriving at Cartagena (Colombia) on 2nd October 1987 for breaking up. [*Daslav Petricio/Malcolm Cranfield collection*]

COMANDANTE CAMILO CIENFUEGOS
In 1962 and 1963 Mambisa took delivery of three of the B54 class ships from Poland. *Comandante Camilo Cienfuegos* lasted until early 1988 when, under the name of *Ciudad de Cienfuegos*, she made a single voyage from Cuba to Chittagong for breaking up. Sister ship *Aracelio Iglesias* was wrecked in 1970 on a voyage from Cuba to Haiphong with a cargo of sugar while *Comandante Andreas Gonzales*, renamed *Gonzales Lines* on delivery, was broken up near Cadiz in 1987. *Comandante Camilo Cienfuegos* was photographed downbound on the St. Lawrence River off Verchères in December 1977. [*Marc Piché/ Malcolm Cranfield collection*]

CARLOS MANUEL DE CESPEDES

In 1975/6 Mambisa took delivery of four new ships of the SD14 type from Austin and Pickersgill. *Carlos Manuel de Cespedes* was photographed arriving at Liverpool on 8th March 1986. Transferred to the Maltese flag in 1989 and renamed *Avon* (while sister ship *Moncada* became the *Severn*), she was sold in 1998 to Roxford Enterprises S.A., a company linked with Canadian Global Sea Carriers Inc., to become *Canadian Pioneer*. Detained at Lagos at the end of 1998, she then disappeared after a reported sale to Bangladesh breakers. As *Pride of the South*, *Moncada* was also ill fated, being attacked by Tamil rebels in 2001 and broken up two years later. *[Malcolm Cranfield]*

CALIXTO GARCIA

The Cuban Government in 1980 purchased two second-hand SD14s from Trinder, Anderson and Co.: the *Ajana*, renamed *Calixto Garcia*, and *Australind*, renamed *Maximo Gomez*, both being named after 19th century generals. *Calixto Garcia*, photographed at Montréal on 22nd November 1989, had her name shortened to *Calix* in 1995, Belize-flagged but still Cuban-owned. Sold in 1997 to Roxford Enterprises S.A., a company linked with Canadian Global Sea Carriers Inc., and renamed *Canadian Challenger*, she sailed from Hamburg for Havana in June 1999 but then disappeared. In a 2003 Canadian court case Roxford had taken legal action against Cuba in connection with *Calix*. *[René Beauchamp/Malcolm Cranfield collection]*

NORTH ISLANDS

North Islands, photographed in the Welland Canal on 19th June 1994 bound for Cuba from Thunder Bay, was the last of four 'Mark 4' SD14s built by Smith's Dock at Middlesbrough and delivered to Cuba during 1986 and 1987. These followed the purchase of two others, named *Lilac Islands* and *Lotus Islands*, after the collapse of the Carrian Group. Although operated by Mambisa, the *North Islands*, *South Islands*, *East Islands* and *West Islands* carried unique funnel colours containing the letters N, S, E and W respectively. Subsequently painted with what became a broadly standard Cuban green hull colour, *North Islands* was wrecked near San Antonio, Chile, on 7th September 1997. *[Barry Anderson/Malcolm Cranfield collection]*

REDESTOS

Two SD14 variants purchased second hand in 1983 by the Cuban Government, named *Redestos* and *Pamit C.*, were among the many ships which, in order to circumvent U.S. sanctions, were flagged out and, from 1994, managed by the recently created Naviera Poseidon. The former Dutch owned *Waterland*, built in 1974, *Redestos* was photographed at Birkenhead on 28th October 1987 in anonymous colours. She arrived at Haiphong on 1st September 1998 as *Queen Bee* to be broken up after a reported sale to Indian breakers fell through leading to her idling in Vietnam waters from April 1997. *[Malcolm Cranfield]*

ODELIS

Odelis, as *Sunderland Venture*, was the last SD14 to be launched at Sunderland, on 17th November 1983. Owned by Wah Kwong of Hong Kong, the ship was in 1985 chartered long-term to Cuba, trading as *Rose Islands* until purchased by Cuba in 1999 and renamed *Odelis*, managed by Naviera Poseidon. Seen in attractive colours passing Portishead on 18th February 2000, *Odelis* was laid up at Havana in 2002 and, after a reported sale for breaking up fell through, sold to Greece in 2005. Taking the name *Theofilos S.* until 2007, and then *Marpessa E.*, she continued trading until sold for breaking up in north west India early in 2013. *[Malcolm Cranfield]*

LAS VILLAS

The second of four ships ordered in 1957 by the Baptista-led Cuban government from Atlantic Shipbuilding at Newport, Monmouthshire, *Las Villas* was delivered in 1959 and managed from 1961 by Mambisa. Photographed at anchor off Montréal in April 1970, *Las Villas* was wrecked on 2nd March 1985 on a loaded voyage between Cartagena, Colombia and Puerto Cabello. *[Marc Piché/ Malcolm Cranfield collection]*

PEPITO TEY

The formerly Finnish-owned *Hansa*, built at Oskarshamn in 1961 and chartered long-term to Transatlantic Carriers Ltd. (Canatlantic Ltd.), was purchased by Cuba in 1972 and managed by Mambisa but flagged out to Somalia under the name of *Marble Islands*. She was one of nine ships purchased between 1970 and 1973 which followed that pattern. One of three ships transferred to the Cuban flag in the mid 1970s, the other two being *Jade Islands* and *Coral Islands*, *Marble Islands* became *Pepito Tey* as which she is seen anchored off Montréal in September 1980. The ship's name was abbreviated to *Tey* for the voyage to breakers in mid-1987, loading cargo at Durres for Port Sudan before moving to Gadani Beach for demolition in December that year. *[Marc Piché/ Malcolm Cranfield collection]*

AGATE ISLANDS

Agate Islands, built at Oskarshamn in 1959 as *Brott* for Norwegian owners, was purchased by Cuba early in 1973 but flagged out to Somalia under the nominal ownership of the Blue Sea Shipping Co. Managed by Mambisa, aided by its London-based agents Empresa Cubana de Fletes ('Cuflet'), *Agate Islands* is seen at London on 30th September 1973. In 1979, in common with several other flagged-out Cuban owned ships, the ship's fleet managers became the Nippon Caribbean Shipping Co. of Tokyo. *Agate Islands* was broken up at Puerto de Santa Maria near Cadiz in March 1986. *[Ian Stockbridge/Malcolm Cranfield collection]*

VIETNAM HEROICO

Photographed at Barbados on 6th October 1978, Mambisa's 1957 Rotterdam-built cargo liner *Vietnam Heroico*, the former *Prins der Nederlanden* which had been purchased by Cuba in 1973, was at the time largely trading to Angola. Apparently laid up at Havana from the end of 1979, *Vietnam Heroico* capsized while under repair on 1st October 1984 and was later broken up at Mamonal, Colombia. *[The late Norman Hesketh]*

RUBEN MARTINEZ VILLENA

One of Mambisa's five Dnepr-type ships built at Kherson between 1978 and 1983, *Ruben Martinez Villena* was photographed sailing from Avonmouth on 20th November 1992. Sold to Greece towards the end of 1993 and renamed *Armonicos*, after a number of name and ownership changes she arrived at Chittagong on 19th November 2008 as *Tarusa* to be broken up. *[Malcolm Cranfield]*

PRIMROSE ISLANDS

One of two bulk carriers built by Austin and Pickersgill in 1982 for the Carrian Group, the flagged-out *Primrose Islands*, photographed at Liverpool on 21st March 1986, had traded as *Carrianna Primrose* and then *Sea Primrose* before being purchased by Cuba in 1985. In common with sister ship *Peony Islands*, and several other Cuban-owned ships, by 1994 her fleet managers had become Nordstrand Maritime and Trading Co. of Piraeus who had operated the ship with a Cuban crew until 2002 as *Tammamy H*. After three further name changes the ship was broken up at Alang in November 2011 as *Deviglory1* while the career of *Peony Islands* followed a similar pattern including three years, between 2008 and 2011, under the rather appropriate name of *Fidel*. *[Malcolm Cranfield]*

CUBA

In 1962 the Soviet Union had gifted to Fidel Castro's government a new tanker, delivered in May that year by Rauma-Repola of Finland as *Artsyz*, which was appropriately named *Cuba*. Operated until 1975 by Empresa Consolidada del Petroleo, then by Empresa de Nav. Caribe, she was photographed, possibly for the last time, near Montréal on 4th August 1980. Not subsequently reported as trading internationally, she is believed to have been broken up in the 1990s. *[Marc Piché/ Malcolm Cranfield collection]*

GOLFO DE GUANAHACABIBES
One of four reefers built for Cuba at Kure, Japan, in 1977 and 1978, *Golfo De Guanahacabibes* was operated by Flota Cubana de Pesca until sold in 1996 to become *Polar Reefer*. After three further name changes the ship was beached at Alang on 11th March 2008 to be broken up. She was photographed near Montréal in August 1979. *[Marc Piché/Malcolm Cranfield collection]*

FRIMARO
The former Spanish reefer *Frimar*, built at Valencia in 1966 and sold to Mambisa in 1972, was operated by Naviera Mar America between 1996 and 2006 and was photographed as such sailing from Havana on 28th March 1997. Equasis indicates that, as at the end of 2012, *Frimaro* may still be in service. *[Nigel Jones]*

VICTORIA DE GIRON
Victoria de Giron was photographed approaching the locks at Kiel-Holtenau in August 1987 in ballast from Porkkala/Kantvik in Finland, where she would have discharged a cargo of sugar, bound for Hull to load cargo for Cuba. One of three sister ships delivered to Mambisa in 1969 by the Swedish builder Uddevallavarvet, the others being *Bahia de Cochinos* and *Playa Larga*, she was in 1997 transferred to Naviera Frigorifica Maritima without change of name and in 1998 sold to Indian breakers, being beached at Alang on 13th May 1998 for that purpose. *[Gerhard Fiebiger/Malcolm Cranfield collection]*

LAZARO PENA

Mambisa's *Lazaro Pena*, built at Rijeka in 1977, is seen anchored off Montréal on 8th July 1981. Renamed *Varadero* in 1991, she remained under Mambisa management until transferred to Naviera Poseidon in 1996 and renamed *Pearl Islands*. After arriving at Havana in mid-1998 she was reportedly renamed *Mayelin* before taking the name *Manpok*, owned by the Government of North Korea. On 31st March 1999, during a voyage from Jakarta, *Manpok* was in collision with the Panama-flag container ship *Hyundai Duke* about 500 miles east of Colombo and sank with the loss of 37 lives. *[Malcolm Cranfield collection]*

DUNLIN

Dunlin was continuously Cuban-owned from delivery to Mambisa at Rijeka in 1977 as *Aracelio Iglesias*, under the name of *Areito* between 1990 and 1996, as *Pine Islands* between 1996 and 1998, as *Vivian* in 1998 and finally as *Dunlin* from some point in 1998 or 1999 until beached at Alang on 20th September 2001 to be broken up. Managed by Naviera Poseidon from 1995 until becoming *Dunlin*, as *Areito* she struck a lock wall on the St. Lawrence River in December 1995 and as *Pine Islands* suffered an engine breakdown in the Gulf of St. Lawrence a year later, being towed into Sydney, Nova Scotia where repairs took until well into 1998 due to lack of finance. *Dunlin* was photographed outside Rio de Janiero on 24th March 2000. *[Nigel Jones]*

KAPPARA

Kappara, delivered in 1978 to Mambisa as *30 De Noviembre* and renamed in 1994 on her transfer to the new Coral Container Line operation, was

photographed outbound from Montréal for Havana on 5th April 1997. Coral Container Lines was set up to run some of Mambisa's cargo liner services but the Dutch-based Melbridge Container Line took over their services between Cuba and Europe from 1999 while the

Cuban-owned, Panama-based Melfi Lines took over the Canada service from 2003. *Kappara* became *African Warrior* in 2002 but was broken up in India in April 2003 after loading a cargo of scrap metal at Avonmouth. *[Marc Piché]*

93

GIORITA

Mambisa had in 1988 and 1989 taken delivery of three small container ships from a Shanghai shipyard with the intention of serving the trade to Europe. Named *Sierra Maestra*, *Ernesto Che Guevara* and *Camilo Cienfuegos*, they were in 1990 all flagged-out and renamed *Giorita*, *Energy* and *Albonica* and then in 1995 transferred to Coral Container Lines. Whereas *Sierra Maestra* retained her name of *Giorita*, as here seen sailing from Havana on 26th March 1997, the latter two ships were renamed *Grosserman* and *Gutterman*. All three were sold in 2000, *Giorita* becoming *Amalia* and then *Doowoo Busan* in 2004 before becoming the first of the trio to be broken up, in China during January 2013. *[Nigel Jones]*

HUNTSVILLE

A uniquely Cuban naming policy was to copy the names of ships which had served Cuba in the past, possibly in violation of U.S. sanctions. One such ship was *Huntsville*, named after the 1957-built ship of that name owned by Power Steam Ship Co. Others had included *Huntsland*, *Avis Faith*, *Ravens* and *Olebratt* and possibly also *Redestos* and *Standwear* (sic). Operated by Empresa Cubana de Fletes ('Cuflet') and managed by Nippon Caribbean Shipping Company, this 1972 Japanese-built bulk carrier, delivered as *Mandarin Venture*, was in 1996 transferred to Naviera Poseidon and renamed *Ruby Islands* as which she arrived at Bahia Honda, Cuba, in September 1998 to be broken up. *Huntsville* was photographed at Kiel on 26th March 1994. *[Michael Niedig]*

ALITRIC

This feature would not be complete without one of the many interesting 'Cuflet' charters. *Alitric* had served Cuba from mid-1969 to the end of 1971. Built by William Gray at Hartlepool in 1953 as *Aliki Livanos* and trading as *Tarpon Bay* between 1964 and 1969, *Alitric*, photographed at Montréal in July 1971, arrived at Burriana, Spain on 25th June 1972 to be broken up. *[Marc Piché/Malcolm Cranfield collection]*

MESSAGERIES MARITIMES AND THEIR POST-WAR REBUILDING PROGRAMME: Part 2

Dr Jean-Pierre Burel

Masterpieces: the 9,300-ton G and H classes

The last of the 8,300-ton class was not yet out of the La Ciotat yard when another series was ordered. From the late forties, the Swedes had put their hopes in fast ships, with Transatlantic's *Nimbus* series for the Australian services, and Johnson's *Seattle* for the US West Coast service. This time, British and Japanese competition meant that speed would be the major issue, with an 18-knot plus loaded speed specified from the start. These ships were needed for the ever more competitive East Asia trade, where *Benloyal*, NYK cargo liners and their followers had left their mark, and also for the Australian wool trade, for which speed was essential. Yet what the *Benloyal* lacked was a modern diesel engine, with power in the 10,000 to 15,000 BHP range.

As mentioned earlier, steam was out of the question: Messageries Maritimes having greatly suffered from its post-war steam experiments on the Far East trio of combi liners *Viet-Nam*, *Cambodge*, and *Laos* (constant trouble with the Rateau turbines on the first unit, almost unworkable Velox boilers on the second, meaning that a six-year-old ship had to be re-boilered by 1961, and catastrophic auxiliaries on all three!).

On single-screw ships, motive power could now be provided by 10-cylinder, Sulzer RSAD 76 engines, or with the 11-cylinder, Burmeister & Wain 1174VTBF160. The whole series came in two batches, five with Sulzers, and another five with Burmeister & Wain engines, depending on the builder's ability to deliver at such short notice (CCM Mantes for Sulzers - deemed by company engineers as building the Rolls-Royce of marine engines - and Forges et Ateliers du Creusot for Burmeister machinery). Another change was the uniform use of 220 volts DC current as opposed to 110 volts continuous current on earlier units.

Whilst the whole series was ordered from three yards, Chantiers et Ateliers de Provence, at Port de Bouc, and Chantiers de La Ciotat, the tenth and final unit was subcontracted to Cockerill

Ougrée at Antwerp and was to all intents and purposes the best of the lot.

There was no radical redesign of the accommodation, with the distinctive extended bridge retained: only the hull showed significant differences because the 18-knot speed called for a complete redesign, with many model experiments at the Wageningen tank. Yet changes were kept to a minimum, and revolutionary measures such as bulbous bows or open stern frames were left to more progressive lines. In fact, modifications in dimensions were dictated by a different block coefficient (a 90 cm widening; 110cm in *Vivarais*, and an overall length increased to 156.5 metres), and by a significantly longer engine room. Hull shapes were refined,

with pronounced flare forward (which gave rise to pronounced slamming in any head seas), together with slimmer lines forward and aft. Some compensation for this lost volume in the hulls was found in an extended forecastle over number 1 hold, giving three large 'tween decks forward, and in the event both number 3 'tween decks remained refrigerated.

Accommodation was yet again revised, this time for four passengers in one luxury, twin-bedded cabin with an en-suite sitting room, and another twin-bedded cabin. The extensive forward lounge was suppressed, and the captain's dining room was provided with an attendant 'fumoir'. The captain's accommodation was moved to the space freed below the bridge,

G-type

Name	Date	Grt/Dwt	Builders	Subsequent history
Maori	12.1958	7,474/ 9,400	Chantiers de La Ciotat	1971: sprang a leak whilst carrying nickel and sank; 38 dead, 1 survivor.
Marquisien	6.1959	7,474/ 9,400	Chantiers de La Ciotat	1978: *Patricia S* (Pan). 1984: b/u Gadani Beach.
Malais	8.1959	7,474/ 9,600	Chantiers de La Ciotat	1978: *Brunella* (Pan). 1984: b/u Alang.
Mauricien	3.1960	7,474/ 9,400	Chantiers de La Ciotat	1978: CTL after collision, b/u Taiwan.
Martiniquais	6.1960	7,475/ 9,400	Chantiers de La Ciotat	1978: *Rafaella* (Pan). 1981: CTL Mombasa, b/u in situ.

H-type

Name	Date	Grt/Dwt	Builders	Subsequent history
Vosges	9.1960	7,508/ 9,450	Ateliers & Chantiers de Provence, Port de Bouc.	1978: *Paulina* (Gr). 1978: *Forum Express* (Gr). 1982: *Al Montaseer* (Saudi). 1982: sank after fire.
Ventoux	1.1961	7,508/ 9,450	Ateliers & Chantiers de Provence, Port de Bouc.	1978: *Corinna* (Gr). 1984: b/u Mumbai.
Vivarais	1961	7,504/ 9,420	Cockerill Ougrée, Hoboken.	1978: *White Rose* (Hon). 1982: laid up. 1985: b/u Shanghai.
Vanoise	5.1961	7,508/ 9,308	Chantiers de La Ciotat	8.1972: lengthened 18.8 m by Lisnave.
Velay	8.1961	7,508/ 9,450	Chantiers de La Ciotat	10.1972: lengthened 18.8 m by Lisnave.

with a comfortable lounge and en suite office and bedroom. The rest of the accommodation remained much the same, except for a few stairs that were moved around, an infirmary relocated to the after end of shelter deck and, of course, last but not least, the provision of full air conditioning throughout the accommodation. Building methods remained unchanged, and cargo handling arrangements were exactly the same as on the 8,300-ton class.

As such the ships were capable of over 20 knots on trials and sustained over 19 knots in service. On endurance trials *Velay* was credited with a loaded speed of 19.7 knots on a daily consumption of 42 tons of boiler fuel.

Certain features allowed different ships in the series to be recognised; for instance *Maori* and *Marquisien* lacked the wide accommodation for chief engineers and chief officers that the others were given. The V-type did not carry a whaler on the port side, whilst only the *Vivarais* had vertical stanchions to her outer decks. These ships were the post-war masterpieces of the fleet and very few new features could now be added.

The full quintet of G types. Top: *Marquisien* on 25th February 1973 in Otago Harbour. *[J. and M. Clarkson]* Middle: *Malais* at Gibraltar in 1969. *[J.and M. Clarkson]* and the ill-fated *Maori* which sank on 9th November 1971. *[F.W. Hawks]*. Whilst homeward bound from Noumea, about 36 hours from Le Havre, she sprang a leak and listed 20 degrees to starboard, causing her cargo of nickel ingots to shift. After an explosion when the list reached 45 degrees, she sank some 500 miles west of La Pallice. The rescue attempt was botched, and it took seven hours to reach the site of the casualty, by when there was just one survivor, the Fourth Engineer. Bottom: *Mauricien [Tom Rayner/J. and M. Clarkson]* and *Martiniquais [Russell Priest]*.

The super-Vs (I-type) and the container problem

For the last three ships, the 'super-Vs', Messageries Maritimes followed the general trend by building repeats but giving them automated engine rooms and providing bridge control of their Sulzer 14,000-BHP 9RD76 machinery. The planned complement was reduced accordingly to 24 (instead of the customary 40 to 45), giving rise, as ever in France, to prolonged strikes, and protracted negotiations on manning levels: the head count finally stopping at 26. Yet these three ships were merely refinements of their forerunners, with improved accommodation (formica and other plastic surfaces being another trend, and single cabins for everyone), and some defects finally corrected, such as a relative weakness in following seas, the ships being given an enclosed stern.

The H-types as completed. Top: *Ventoux. [Roy Fenton collection]*. Middle: *Vosges [Russell Priest]* and *Vivarais. [J. and M. Clarkson]*. Bottom: *Vanoise* 2nd April 1971 in Otago Harbour *[J. and M. Clarkson]* and *Velay [Roy Fenton collection]*.

The deck department's work was simplified by adopting automated Macgregor single-pull hatch covers, with hydraulic folding covers in each level of the number 3 hold. The only significant changes to the design were to the bridge and the arrangements for central control of the main engine. Chart room and bridge were merged into a 'salle nautique', whilst not widely open at the sides (because of the traditionally wide enclosed bridge), this was the command centre of the ship. In the engine rooms provisions were made for an air-conditioned, sound-proofed, auxiliary control room. The whole of the accommodation block remained much as it had been designed ten years earlier, except for moving the mess to starboard. Yet stability was a problem as ever, with no provision for liquid ballast tanks: a feature not provided until the Z units a decade later.

This was the fleet at the end of 1965: three *Iraouaddys*, ten 8,300-tonners, ten 9,300-tonners, and three 'super-Vs'. Older units had gone, Liberties to the French state, which quickly sold them for further service, and most of the *Mékong* class sold en bloc to Djakarta Lloyd, together with *Donaï*.

At the end of this programme, the company's president in a press conference held on board *Ferdinand de Lesseps* mooted the intention of ordering a totally new series for the Far East from Chantiers de la Ciotat (a series which would eventually emerge as the 'Explorateurs' class of Compagnie Maritime Chargeurs Réunis), but in the event nothing came to pass, at least for Messageries Maritimes.

Meanwhile, the French Government sent Messageries Maritimes on a rescue attempt: that of the Sud-Atlantique and Chargeurs Réunis passenger services to South America. Absorbing the three remaining combi liners and taking over Compagnie de Navigation d'Orbigny for freight carrying, and finally converting the new

I-type

Name	Date	Grt/Dwt	Builders	Subsequent history
Var	9.1964	7,594/9,480	Chantiers de La Ciotat	11.1972: lengthened 18.5 m by Lisnave.
Vienne	12.1964	7,595/9,480	Chantiers de La Ciotat	6.1972: lengthened 18.5 m by Lisnave.
Vaucluse	3.1965	7,594/9,480	Chantiers de La Ciotat	7.1972: lengthened 18.5 m by Lisnave.

The I type *Var*. [Robert Scott]

Vienne as built, photographed on 18th August 1971. [J. and M. Clarkson]

Vaucluse as built. [J. and M. Clarkson]

flagship intended for the Pacific, for an en bloc replacement of those combi liners, absorbed all the resources available at a critical time when there was a dire need for tonnage. No new buildings could be afforded until 1970, when the passenger fleet withdrawal was complete. But by then there had been the advent of the beautiful Ben Line cargo ships, and ever more progressive Nordic and Japanese types. Yet, far more dangerous, sparked by men like Malcolm McLean and Marshall Meek, the container revolution had come. The rest of the tale need not be told!

Messageries Maritimes tried to join TRIO, a consortium with Ben Line, Chargeurs Réunis, and later Compagnie Maritime Belge. The SMEFEO service was an aborted attempt to keep at bay the Scandutch services. But in the end the long laid-up *Korrigan*, which replaced no less than ten cargo ships at a stroke, had to be used and Messageries Maritimes lost its soul in the Scandutch Pool. Australian services also went the same way, with entry into the AECS pool, yet with a La Ciotat-built ship, this time *Kangourou*.

Meanwhile, five old units were stretched, rather discreetly in Portuguese Lisnave yards. Thus the 'super-Vs', *Vanoise* and *Velay*, were lengthened by 18.80 metres and equipped with powerful 25-ton ASEA cranes able to handle 44 containers. A couple of 10-ton derricks were also placed on the superstructure front. And the ships soldiered on right until the end. Chargeurs did the same with the stretching of their C-type in German yards, giving them Stülcken heavy-lift derricks.

And that is the end of the tale. Afterwards came only accountants and spin doctors making the illness even worse, by ill-thought-out diversification projects into bulk, gas, and very large crude carriers. Sometimes, what you learn in school allows only for pre-set disasters: only experience, resilience, and sticking to core business tells!

H-type

Name	Date	Grt/Dwt	Builders	Subsequent history
Vanoise	8.1972	7,769/11,662	Lisnave	1979: *Char Ly* (Taiwan). 1983: *Magida* (Saudi). 1983: b/u Taiwan.
Velay	10.1972	7,769/11,662	Lisnave	1979: *Char Hang* (Taiwan). 1982: *Samira* (Saudi). 1982: *Largish No.4.* (Pan). 1984: b/u Taiwan.

Vanoise after lengthening. *[FotoFlite incorporating Skyfotos, 201243]*

Velay as lengthened. *[Ian Shiffman]*

I-type lengthening

Name	Date	New GRT/Dwt	By	Subsequent history
Var	11.1972	7,799/11,840	Lisnave	1979: *Char Yeung* (Taiwan). 1982: *Fawzia* (Saudi). 1982: *Largish No.1.* (Pan). 1984: b/u Taiwan.
Vienne	6.1972	7,799/11,840	Lisnave	1979: *Char Kang* (Taiwan). 1982: *Wakheed* (Saudi) 1982: *Largish No.2.* (Pan). 1984: b/u Taiwan
Vaucluse	7.1972	7,799/11,840	Lisnave	1981: *Char Kwei* (Panama). 1984: b/u Taiwan.

Three further views of the lengthened I class. Top: *Var. [Trevor Jones/Russell Priest]*

Middle: *Vienne. [Marc Piche/Russell Priest]*

Bottom: *Vaucluse. [Fotoflite incorporating Skyfotos, 201288]*

All three lengthened I types were eventually sold to the Char Ching Marine Co. Ltd. of Taiwan. This is the former *Var* well loaded with containers as the *Char Yeung* of a Panama-based subsidiary. *[FotoFlite incorporating Skyfotos, 325700]*

Sailing with the Messageries Maritimes

Sailing with the Messageries was an experience, and one which none of today's cruise ships can equal. We were on Imperial Service ships, with a tradition dating back to 1865. Service was inherited from first class on the mail ships, and was extended to all officers being allowed to bring wives and children on board. Sailing for families was gradually extended from the Mediterranean, i.e. from not sailing the Gibraltar Straits, to sailing for the whole coastal trip, from the first unloading port (generally Marseilles) to the last loading harbour (generally La Pallice after the Suez closure, sometimes Genoa or Livorno). And coasting would go as far as Hamburg: yet there were no coastal crews, crew members being replaced progressively when reaching French harbours (typically Marseilles, Le Havre and Dunkirk).

On board prevailed first class service for officers, with uniformed Comorian 'garçons', starched linen and plenty of silverware recovered from the mail ships. Finally, even the libraries came from mail ships. A bell would summon us to the meal table at 12:00 and 19:00 in harbour, slightly offset by a quarter of an hour at sea, giving officers time to change into dark blue uniforms. Lesser ranks would be

called at 11:30 and 18:30, just the same, giving kitchen staff time for the officer's service. There was no bell for tea time yet it too was fully attended, and came at 16:00, although uniforms were not usually worn for the occasion. Down on the shelter deck there were other rituals to observe, such as the 10:00 pause, during which red wine was substituted for coffee, although served in regulation coffee cups (Pyllevuit tableware). As ever, neckties were compulsory and, more often than not, dining room access was denied to those who refused to wear them!

Beds and cabins were cleaned on a daily basis for the officers, less often for lower ranks, but breakfast and tea continued to be brought (usually to the master, chief mate, and chief engineer) on silver trays right until the end.

Dining arrangements, as ever in France, were complicated; with no less than five dining rooms on board. On the port side of the passenger deck ate, in secluded calm, the master, chief engineer and chief officer (to whom loading operations were entirely delegated). Starboard side was the junior officers' abode, under the watchful eye of the second engineer (he was after all 'président de carré'), all this requiring no less than three waiters: one for the captain's dining room, one

for the officers, and one for pantry work. Traditionally, the captain offered a cocktail to all officers in the officers' dining room or lounge on Sundays.

On the shelter deck, crews had their meals in the 'refectoire', served by a special waiter, called the 'postal'. Just aft, mates had their own dining room for the bosun, assistant bosun ('second maître'), bidel (the ship's writer, who was in fact the chief officer's secretary), 'intendant', carpenter, electrician and head greaser. Later, there was a third service for all kitchen staff, i.e. chief cook, assistant cook, baker and the 'postal'. Pastries would be offered to all crew members on thursdays and sundays, and a party complete with roast would be held on the long-hauls outwards and homewards.

It should be mentioned in passing that French ships never had chief stewards: in their place sat the first officer, or 'lieutenant commissaire', in command of the wages and the custom goods (i.e. tax free items sold on board to the crew), and in turn controlled the 'intendant' who, whilst not ranking as an officer, had a big say in the day-to-day running of the hotel services and expenses: this was undoubtedly reminiscent of the old-time castles. The second officer was in charge of navigation, chart upkeep, and security. Sometimes a junior second would be

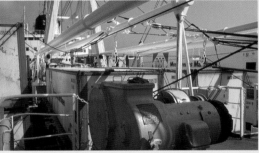

The photographs on this page were taken on the *Vanoise* by Captain Charles Protat, during a westbound, round-the-world sailing on the Scandutch service in 1972. Outwards the voyage took the nearly new *Vanoise* via Panama and Hawaii, whilst she came home via Cape Town. *[Captain Charles Protat]*

embarked whilst on the coastal run, thus relieving the chief officer of his watches.

Crews were remarkably homogeneous, when not analysed by the scale set by the Marseilles mail ships. Officers came generally from Brittany and Normandy with the odd transfer from Marseilles, where a spell on liners meant promotion to senior rank. Mates usually came from Brittany. The small island of Ushant in the Channel has to be mentioned as it provided most of the line's bosuns. Deck crews generally came from Brittany, with again a few transfers from the Marseilles region. The engine room staff was more interesting; Breton head greasers and electricians, with a motley group of generally illiterate members coming from the old West African colonies (with officers often needing to step in when it came to writing to families or sending money home). Most were Moslems yet religious issues never seem to have had much impact on crews ('jambon' was totally dissociated from ham and pork in those days!). Restaurant personnel were recruited from the whole of France when it came to chief steward, bakers and chefs, yet service personnel were rather different: 'postals' were generally from East Africa or more often disabled sailors, whilst 'salle à manger' and

pantry crew were inevitably Comorian. Strangely, very few crew members came from Asia, a potent testimony to the conflict that had gone on there.

In conclusion, the examination of the trip report must be mentioned, as this was where the real sense of 'expedition maritime' - a synonym in French law for a ship's voyage - had its full meaning. All cargo ships were run from Dunkirk, where the ships were repaired. This meant that every ship returning home was the subject to a very careful enquiry on the 'rapport de voyage' (trip report: a 20-page document covering all aspects of navigation, time spent in port, commercial aspects of the various destinations, crewing and loading, with detailed descriptions from the master, the chief officer, chief engineer and purser. This report covered every department with anything from oil to everyday wine consumption and, of course, an appreciation of every member of the crew, which reflected the atmosphere prevailing on board, and which was vital for any ascension of the promotion ladder. Thus the master reported on all officers, including those in the engine room department, except for the lower ranks. The chief officer reported on the deck department, and finally the 'lieutenant commissaire'

(i.e. purser) reported on the activities of the hotel department. This enquiry was conducted upon arrival in Dunkirk by the 'capitaine d'armement' (marine superintendant), delegates from Services Techniques and catering firms (SHRM), and shore repair firms, together with the master, chief officer and chief engineer. This meant a particularly long afternoon for any officer who presented his ship rust streaked or otherwise damaged. Cleanliness was paramount, since most working hours on the homeward leg were used in painting the ship inside and out. Outwards, only rigging was checked, except on the New Zealand run where stevedores imposed cleanliness standards which were generally loathed by crews. Strangely, when repairs required more serious work, such as steel replacement and sandblasting the hull, they were carried out in Hamburg, to the general pleasure of the crews, assured of prolonged night visits to Sankt Pauli and the Reeper Bahn.

Thus was the atmosphere of the Messageries Maritimes' post-war fleet, with its simplified white and black colour scheme, a company so proud of its unicorn emblem that it never bothered to advertise on its own funnels.

Nomen, numen, said the ancient Latins. Messageries applied the motto to the full.

SD14 UPDATE 2014
Simon Smith

At the end of April 2014 there were just three British-built SD14s and one Prinasa 121 still active. Some of the Chinese-owned vessels have disappeared without there being any definite information on their arrival at ship breakers but it would be very surprising if any of these survive. The Hai Phong port website continues to list the *Phuong Mai Star* and *Sunrise 6*, but they may well have been demolished. If any readers can shed any light on their current status it would be greatly appreciated.

The previous SD14 update appeared in 'Record' 46, July 2010.

Phuong Mai Star was launched in 1978 as *Dalworth* by Austin and Pickersgill Ltd. but completed in 1979 as *Song Duong* for Vietnam Ocean Shipping Co. (VOSCO). Photographed laid-up at Nha Be on the Saigon River on 26th February 2013, she was subsequently auctioned and arrived at Hai Phong in August 2013. Her current status is unknown. *[Simon Smith]*

Ryong Gang 2 was completed by Austin and Pickersgill for German owners in 1980 as *Globe Trader*. She was photographed at Singapore in November 2010. She is believed to be still trading in 2014. *[John Nunn]*

Yard No.	IMO No.	Completed as	Name as in SD14/Record 46	Flag	Year	Notes
906	7393391	Ormos	Jin Da Hai	CHN	1976	Last AIS Bohai Bay 8.2010. Status unknown but believed demolished.
1377	7610062	Empros	QSM Dubai	PAN	1977	To Indian breakers and arrived Alang 25.1.2011, beached 4.2.2011.
1378	7611559	Cluden	De Sheng	CHN	1978	To Chinese breakers and arrived Jingjiang 18.3.2012.
1380	7611561	Song Duong	Phuong Mai Star	CHN	1979	8.2011 laid-up Saigon River. 8.2013 Arrived Hai Phong. Current status unknown.
1381	7607481	Funing	Zheng Yang 2	CHN	1978	To Chinese breakers and arrived Ningde 20.3.2012.
1383	7607493	Grand Faith	Jin Yuan Hu	CHN	1980	To Di Gang Shipbreaking and arrived Wuhu 24.9.2012.
1384	7611573	Thai Binh	Dong Binh	VNM	1980	To Vietnamese breakers and demolition began at Hai Phong prior to 13.3.2013.
1385	7614719	Bronte	Jin Cheng Xin 8	CHN	1979	To Chinese breakers and arrived Xinhui 2.11.2011.
1387	7614733	Browning	Dae San	PRK	1979	3.2013 Renamed Ocean Dawn (Cambodian flag) for Hubao Marine Ltd. To Bangladeshi breakers and arrived Chittagong 20.4.2013, beached 9.5.2013.
1389	7614757	Boswell	He Ping 28	CHN	1979	Last AIS off Hong Kong 20.2.2009. Status unknown but believed demolished
1390	7614769	To Lich	Sturdy Falcon	VNM	1980	To Indian breakers and arrived Alang 10.1.2012, beached 21.1.2012.
1391	7614771	Belloc	Nadeen	TZA	1980	Trading with cement Karachi/Iraq 2014.
1394	7640354	Good Faith	He Feng	PAN	1979	Trading China/Solomon Islands 2014.
1395	7640366	Future Hope	Jin Cheng Xin 6	CHN	1979	To Chinese breakers and arrived Zhangjiagang 14.1.2011.
1396	7640378	Globe Trader	Ryong Gang 2	PRK	1980	Trading North Korea/China 2014.
1397	7628423	Darya Lok	Alkawther	SLE	1980	To Indian breakers and arrived Alang 14.1.2011, beached 20.1.2011.
1400	7822380	Jade Ii	Golden Light	VNM	1980	To Vietnamese breakers and arrived Hai Phong 30.3.2013.

Golden Light was built by Austin and Pickersgill in 1978 as *Jade II*. She is seen laid-up on the Saigon River on 26th February 2013. She sailed from there on 13th March 2013 and arrived at a demolition site at Hai Phong on 30th March 2013. *[Simon Smith]*

Far East was completed by Austin and Pickersgill for Hong Kong interests in 1982 as *United Enterprise*. She was photographed at Singapore in 2011, and went to Indian breakers early in 2012. *[Ian Edwards]*

1401	7628411	Jade III	Phuc Hai 5	VNM	1980	To Vietnamese breakers. Demolition began at Hai Phong prior to 30.9.2012.
1403	8000159	Hun Jiang	Zheng Yang 3	CHN	1981	Laid-up off Dalian 5.2012 to 9.2012. Current status unknown
1414	8011768	Yuan Jiang	Jin Yuan Shan	CHN	1981	To Di Gang Shipbreaking and arrived Wuhu 28.11.2012.
1415	8102086	United Enterprise	Far East	VNM	1982	To Indian breakers and arrived Sachana 10.1.2012.
1417	8102103	United Drive	Fortress 7	TGO	1982	To Xin Min Shipbreaking and arrived Jingjiang 17.12.2013.
1418	8102115	United Spirit	Hyang Ro Bong	PRK	1982	6.4.2011 Partially sank after collision in Chittagong Roads (total loss).
1426	8207953	Sunderland Venture	Marpessa E.	PAN	1985	To Indian breakers and arrived Mumbai 16.2.2013, beached 5.3.2013.
440	7324170	Stephanos Vergottis	Heng Chang Lun	CHN	1973	5.2011 Renamed *Fu Xiang 6* for Chinese owners. To Chinese breakers at Lianyungang (Guanhe River) 2.9.2011.
462	7422790	Sea Lion	Li Yuan He Ping	CHN	1977	To Chinese breakers and arrived Jingjiang 8.9.2011.
463	7422805	Morviken	Hai Ji Shun	CHN	1978	Last AIS Nanjing 31.12.2010. Status unknown but believed demolished
1350	8120739	Carrianna Lotus	Lotus Islands	PAN	1983	2004: Renamed *Weng* for Aqua Azur Shipmanagement B.V. To Chinese breakers and arrived Jingjiang 8.6.2011.
1357	8500965	South Islands	Phuong Dong 3	VNM	1986	10.2011 Renamed *Sunrise 18* (Vietnam flag) for Mai Mai Trading. 1.2013 Grounded off East Java. Wreck still largely intact 1.2014.
1358	8500977	West Islands	Phuong Dong 1	VNM	1986	5.2011 Renamed *Sunrise 6* (Vietnam flag) for Mai Mai Trading. 26.4.2013 Arrived Hai Phong. Current status unknown.

Sunrise 18 was completed by Smith's Dock Co. Ltd. in 1986 for Cuban interests as *South Islands*. The photograph above was taken in the Eastern Anchorage at Singapore on 27th February 2012. In January 2013 she grounded near Tuban, East Java. Although there were plans to break her up *in situ* the wreck remains largely intact (right). The smoke in the background comes from a fire on board the Indonesian products tanker *Providence* (9,738/1986) which occurred during single buoy mooring operations. *[Simon Smith]*

| 1359 | 8500989 | East Islands | Phuong Dong 2 | VNM | 1986 | 11.2010 Renamed Safina 2 (Comoros Islands flag) for Gemini Shipping Pte. Ltd. To Indian breakers and arrived Alang 26.3.2013, beached 9.4.2013. |
| 51 | 7411909 | Presidente Ramon S. Castillo | Presidente Ramon S. Castillo | ARG | 1980 | 1.2011 Remained partially demolished at Ibicuy. |

Another SD14 built by Smith's Dock Co. Ltd. for Cuba, as *East Islands*, *Phuong Dong 2* is in the process of changing her name to *Safina 2* at Singapore on 15th May 2011. She was sold to breakers at Alang in 2013. *[John Nunn]*

127	7433153	Lloyd Marelha	Jing Ren	CHN	1977	Last AIS off Wenzhou 05.6.2009, status unknown but believed demolished
130	7433177	Monte Alto	Fortune Sea	PAN	1979	Last AIS off China 2010, status unknown but believed demolished
141	7433191	Anisio Borges	Fu Sheng 82	CHN	1983	To Chinese breakers and arrived Zhangjiagang 21.3.2013.
143	7433206	Leonor	Nama	PAN	1988	To Indian breakers and arrived Alang 28.1.2012, beached 5.2.2012.
151	7433244	Ana Luisa	Lily Royal	MDV	1981	To Indian breakers and arrived Alang 16.5.2013, beached 30.5.2013.
152	7433256	Lloyd Houston	Jaipur	JOR	1981	To Indian breakers and arrived Mumbai 27.10.2010, beached 4.11.2010.
153	7433268	L/L Brasil	Ra Nam	PRK	1982	To Indian breakers and arrived Alang 22.3.2012, beached 4.4.2012.
156	7433270	Rodrigo	Shipinco I	PAN	1983	To Vietnamese breakers and arrived Hai Phong 15.3.2012.
157	7433202	Alessandra	Lily Noble	MDV	1983	To Indian breakers and arrived Alang 4.9.2013, beached 12.9.2013.

Above: *Shipinco I* was launched in 1982 by Companhia Comercio e Navegacao (CCN) as *Rodrigo*. She is approaching Vung Tau on 28th February 2012 having sailed from Saigon for ship breakers at Hai Phong after a period of lay-up. *[Simon Smith]* Below: As these photographs show, there was considerable variation in the cargo gear fitted to Brazilian-built SD14s. *Lily Noble* of 1983 was photographed at Singapore on 13th March 2013 six months before she went to the breakers. *[Both: John Nunn]*

Another version of the Brazilian SD14 with a mixture of cranes and conventional derricks, *Ryu Gyong* is seen at Singapore. She was broken up in China during 2012. *[John Nunn]*

158	7433294	Lloyd Venezuela	Ryu Gyong	PRK	1983	6.2011: Renamed O SONG SAN for Korea O Song Shipping Co. 8.2011 Renamed GLORY (Mongolian flag) for Glory Shipping Ltd. To Chinese breakers and arrived Tianjin 6.8.2012.
159	7433309	Renata	Mercs Mihintale	LKA	1983	To Indian breakers and arrived Alang 13.7.2010, beached 23.7.2010.
160	7802976	Tucurui	Yi Yiang 1	CHN	1988	To Chinese breakers and arrived Fu'An 1.2012.

Amar (above and top of next page) is one of just two surviving Brazilian-built derivatives of the SD14, the Prinasa-121. She was photographed in derelict condition off Batam on 9th August 2012. *[John Nunn]*

| 134 | 7432903 | *Frotadurban* | *Amar* | --- | 1980 | 2.2014 Anchored in derelict condition off Batam. |
| 155 | 7432953 | *Frotasingapore* | *Man Pung* | PRK | 1982 | Trading North Korea/China 2014. 4.2014 Renamed ANA (Tuvalu flag) for Integrity Ships Pte. Ltd. |

Photographed at Singapore, *Man Pung* is the only Prinasa 121 still trading. *[John Nunn]*
Copies of 'SD14: The Full Story' remain available from Ships in Focus at £14.75 plus postage.

SHIPS' BROCHURES:
SWEDISH A CLASS REEFERS 1964-1965
Tony Breach

During the 1960s demands for fresh fruits, meats and seafood in the northern hemisphere were increasing as the world recovered from the effects of the conflict of the 1940s. Britain had a reasonably adequate fleet of refrigerated cargo liners well capable of carrying finished goods for export to Commonwealth and other southern hemisphere countries, returning with refrigerated foodstuffs to British and North European ports; an ideal trading arrangement. The Scandinavian nations, as cross-traders, saw the opportunity of building and operating handy dedicated ships for food transportation. Their major players were the ship owners J. Lauritzen of Denmark who had pre-war experience with refrigerated ships and the Swedish Salen organisation which had working experience with the banana importer Carl Matthiessens.

This article concerns the Transatlantic company of Gothenburg as well as the Salen company whose connection with bananas started in 1922, distributing bananas by sea within Europe and serving Stockholm, Gothenburg, Copenhagen and Oslo. It is interesting to note that the early ships involved in these northerly climes were insulated and heated, rather than refrigerated, as was also the case with specialised banana wagons on north European railways. In 1941 Salen took delivery of the *Sandhamn*, their first reefer, a small motor ship of 3,090 deadweight tons and 183,400 cubic feet refrigerated cargo space, and between 1952 and 1963 they built eleven reefers and acquired a further five second hand. In 1964 the first of a batch of six modem motor reefers was ordered from Eriksbergs Mekaniska Verksted A/B of Gothenburg of which four were to be managed and operated by Salenrederierna of Stockholm and two were to be managed and operated by Rederi A/B Transatlantic of Gothenburg. There were important

financial links between the owning parties which were not unusual at that time, particularly in Scandinavia, and these are indicated in the vessels' histories.

M/S "ANTILOPE"

SALÉNREDERIERNA
(SALÉN SHIPPING COMPANIES)

STOCKHOLM 14
SWEDEN

TELEGRAMS: SAILING
TELEPHONE: 679760
TELEX: 1627 SAILING STH

Brochures

While refrigerated cargo liners were reconfigurable common carriers, reefers were a dedicated type and, if not owned by fruit companies, they depended predominantly upon time charters, generally with banana companies, for employment. The contemporary vessel-owning banana companies had a preference for a moderate-sized core fleet supplemented by time or occasionally voyage charters, while the seasonal fruit shippers favoured voyage or very short time charters. For the independent reefer operator it was therefore necessary to advertise his tonnage in the most attractive manner and at this the Scandinavians showed their competence. While this article features only the brochure for the lead vessel of the group, each of the vessels had a similar brochure and, in the case of the two Transatlantic ships, the brochure went as far as giving, in addition to manufacturers' details

of all items of on-board equipment, their serial numbers. Unashamed salesmanship! It is important to understand that the brochures gave any potential charterer complete information about a particular vessel and that he therefore might be expected to fully understand the probable performance of that vessel while in his service; a very important consideration when dealing with perishable commodities. Whether or not the brochure was a form of implied warranty or whether it was ever attached to a charter party is outside the knowledge of the writer. Over the years the brochures became more detailed and specific and by the time the Salen open hatch 'Winter' class was introduced they were produced as a pocket-book size in sufficient quantities to distribute to agents, stevedores, brokers and to ships' officers for whom it was a very useful tool.

Of particular interest, the brochures show plans of the ship which indicate the unique layout of all reefers. There is also a deadweight scale, capacity information for cargo compartments, ballast and fresh water as well as fuel oils and lubricants. Bin capacity refers to the contemporary method of banana stem stowage whereby horizontal portable boards were inserted into semi-permanent wooden pillars to allow for access to fruit and, very importantly, to shell doors for securing on completion of loading in the A decks. Bale capacity was applicable when the bins were removed for other commodities or bananas in cartons.

A note on tonnages.

The tonnages given are those in the original brochures. During their lives these vessels saw, amongst other things, changes in tonnage measurements including alternative tonnages as well as measurement changes due to transfers to different flags.

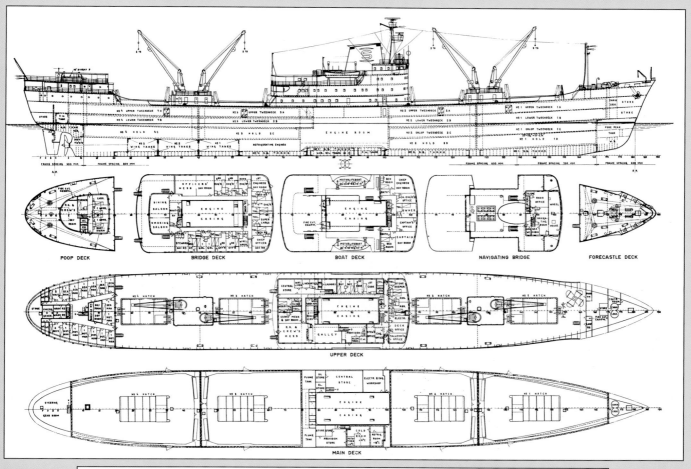

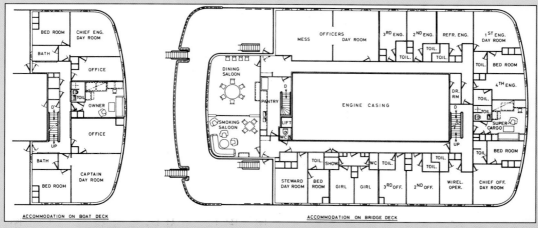

ACCOMMODATION ON BOAT DECK

ACCOMMODATION ON BRIDGE DECK

Above: General arrangement drawing and accommodation plans from the *Antilope's* brochure. *[Author's collection]*

Ariel, fourth member of the class, in Salen colours. *[FotoFlite incorporating SkyFotos, 319510]*

1. ANTILOPE

IMO 5423283 8,239g 8,000d.
149.21 o.l./137.17 b.p. x 18.90 x 9.36 metres.
Refrigerated capacity: 371,060 cubic feet.
2SCSA 8-cyl. Burmeister & Wain 874-VTBF-160-type oil engine by Eriksbergs Mekaniska Verksted A/B, Eriksberg, Sweden; 10,000 BHP, 19 knots.
29.8.1963: Launched by Eriksbergs Mekaniska Verksted A/B, Eriksberg (Yard No. 580) for Rederiet for m.s. 'Antilope', Stockholm, Sweden (Saleninvest A/B 50%, Rederi A/B Transatlantic 25%, Rederi A/B Transmark 25%) as ANTILOPE.
1.1964: Delivered.
3.1978: Sold to Stuart Shipping Company, Monrovia, Liberia (United Maritime Enterprises Ltd. (James Jacounis), London) and put under the Singapore flag.
1981: Transferred to Sociate Shipping Corporation, Monrovia (United Maritime Enterprises Ltd. (James Jacounis), London) and renamed ANTIPOLIS under the Greek flag.
13.7.1983: Laid up at Sharjah.
12.1983: Sold to Pakistani breakers.
22.1.1984: Departed Sharjah under the Maltese flag.
2.1984: Arrived at Gadani Beach for demolition by Habib Builders Ltd.
18.4.1984: Work commenced.

Antilope in the English Channel (upper) and as the Greek-flagged *Antipolis*, still in Salen colours, at Singapore on 31st March 1982 (lower). *[Top: FotoFlite incorporating SkyFotos 254300, bottom: Chris Howell]*

2. ALBANY

IMO 6400018 8,248g 8,100d. 149.21 o.l./137.17 b.p x 18.90 x 9.36 metres. Refrigerated capacity: 367,670 cubic feet.

2SCSA 8-cyl. Burmeister & Wain 874-VTBF-160-type oil engine by Eriksbergs Mekaniska Verksted A/B, Eriksberg, Sweden; 10,000 BHP, 19 knots.

31.10.1963: Launched by Eriksbergs Mekaniska Verksted A/B, Eriksberg, Sweden (Yard No. 581) for Rederiet for m.s. 'Albany', Gothenburg, Sweden (Rederi A/B Transatlantic 25%, Rederi A/B Transmark 25%, Salenrederierna A/B 50%) as ALBANY.

2.1964: Delivered.

1978: Sold to National Ability Compania Naviera S.A., Panama (Comninos Brothers Shipping Co. S.A., Piraeus, Greece) and renamed AEGEAN REEFER under the Greek flag.

7.1985: Laid up at Sharjah.

2.1986: Reactivated, transferred to Marine System S.A. (International Maritime Transports Association S.A., Piraeus) and renamed MARE 1 under the Panama flag.

30.11.1986: Transferred to Libra Maritime International S.A., Panama (International Maritime Transports Association S.A., Piraeus) and renamed REEFER RIO.

1988: Attained global notoriety when her cargo of frozen meat, which was loaded from the EEC surplus stores, was found to be radio-active due to apparent contamination by the Chernobyl disaster. She was eventually discharged at Flushing and here the majority of her 6,000-ton cargo was found to be within EEC radiation limits.

1989: Managers became International Reefer Services S.A., Piraeus and renamed ITAJAI REEFER under the Panama flag.

7.5.1993: Arrived at Alang anchorage.

20.5.1993: Demolition commenced. One source ('Lloyd's Confidential Index') maintains that this vessel was managed by Comninos Brothers Shipping Co. S.A. under the names listed above from 1978 to 1993.

Top: *Albany* in original condition, with name picked out in gold paint shadowed in blue, a Swedish tradition. *[David Kirby/Russell Priest collection]*
Left: As *Aegean Reefer* at Napier, 19th April 1982. *[Chris Howell]*
Above right: As *Reefer Rio*. *[FotoFlite incorporating Skyfotos, 342900]*

3. ARGONAUT

IMO 6412619 8,247g 8,100d.
149.21 o.l./137.17 b.p. x 18.90 x 9.36
metres.
Refrigerated capacity: 374,510 cubic feet.
2SCSA 8-cyl. Burmeister & Wain
874-VTBF-160-type oil engine by
Uddevallavarvet A/B, Uddevalla, Sweden;
10,000 BHP, 19 knots.
29.4.1964: Launched by Eriksbergs
Mekaniska Verksted A/B, Eriksberg,
Sweden (Yard No. 582) for Rederi A/B
Salenia (Salenrederierna), Stockholm,
Sweden as ARGONAUT.
18.11.1964: Delivered.
1977: Sold to Barba Maritime
Corporation, Monrovia, Liberia (United
Maritime Enterprises Ltd. (James
Jacounis), London) and renamed
ARGONAUT II.
1981: Transferred to Diploma Shipping
Corporation, Monrovia (United Maritime
Enterprises Ltd. (James Jacounis),
London) and renamed ARGONAFTIS
under the Greek flag.
1982: Sold to Ocean Master Shipping
Corporation, Monrovia (Reefer Agencies
Inc., Merksem, Belgium) and renamed
ISLAND PEAK under the Panama flag.
1983: Transferred to Old Crown Shipping
Corporation, Monrovia (Reefer Agencies
Inc., Merksem, Belgium) and renamed
CROWN PEAK under the Panama flag.
10.2.1986: Arrived at Gadani Beach for
demolition.

Top: *Argonaut.* [John Matheson/Russell Priest]
Middle: As *Argonaftis*, Greek-flagged but in Salen colours. [Author's collection]
Bottom: In final condition, as *Crown Peak.* [FotoFlite incorporating Skyfotos 33499]

4. ARIEL

IMO 6401115 8,249g 8,100d
149.21 o.l/137.17 b.p. x 18.90 x 9.36
metres.
Refrigerated capacity 374,510 cubic
feet.
2SCSA 8-cyl. Burmeister & Wain
874-VTBF-160-type oil engine by
Eriksbergs Mekaniska Verksted A/B,
Eriksberg, Sweden; 10,000 BHP, 19
knots.
16.3.1964: Delivered by Eriksbergs
Mekaniska Verksted A/B, Eriksberg
(No. 583) to Rederi A/B Jamaica
(Salenrederierna), Stockholm, Sweden
as ARIEL.
1969: Transferred to Salenrederierna
A/B, Stockholm.
1.7.1975: Transferred to Saleninvest
A/B, Stockholm.
3.1978: Sold to Rodolfo Maritime
Corporation, Monrovia, Liberia (United
Maritime Enterprises Ltd. (James
Jacounis), London) and renamed
ARIEL I under the Singapore flag.
1981: Sold to Regina Maritime
Corporation, Monrovia (United
Maritime Enterprises Ltd. (James
Jacounis), London) and renamed
ATHOS I.
1983: Laid up in River Fal.
1984: Sold to Axe Shipping Co. Ltd.,
Malta and renamed PATHOS.
1984: Sold to Transmediterranean
Reefer Carriers S.A., Panama (Overseas
Reefer Carriers S.A., Piraeus, Greece)
and renamed YUKON REEFER.
21.12.1984: Arrived Gadani Beach for
demolition.

Top: *Ariel.* [*Savid Kirby/Russell Priest*]
Middle: *Ariel* as *Athos I*, retaining Salen colours. [*Chris Howell*]
Bottom: A somewhat weary looking *Yukon Reefer* during her last year in service.
[*FotoFlite incorporating Skyfotos 294420*]

5. ARAWAK
IMO 6420329 8,239g 8,100d.
149.21 o.l./137.17 b.p. x 18.90 x 9.36 metres.
Refrigerated capacity 373,610 cubic feet.
2SCSA 8-cyl. Burmeister & Wain 874-VTBF-160-type oil engine by Uddevallavarvet A/B, Uddevalla, Sweden; 10,000 BHP, 19 knots

9.8.1964: Launched by Eriksbergs Mekaniska Verksted A/B, Eriksberg, Sweden (No.588) for Rederiet for m.s. 'Arawak', Stockholm, Sweden (Rederei A/B Salen 50%, Rederi A/B Transatlantic 50%) as ARAWAK.
18.2.1965: Delivered.
1978: Transferred to Saleninvest A/B, Stockholm.

6.1978: Sold to Deanfield Shipping Co. Ltd., Hamilton, Bermuda (Regal Marine Inc., Piraeus, Greece) and renamed ALTCAR.
21.8.1983: Laid up at Brunei Bay, Borneo.
4.7.1984: Arrived Kaohsiung from Brunei Bay for demolition by Chien Yu Steel Industrial Co.

Top: *Arawak* in Rederi A/B Transatlantic colours, but with an atypically scruffy hull. *[Russell Priest]*
Bottom: *Arawak* as *Altcar*, now in Salen colours. *[FotoFlite incorporating Skyfotos 4299]*

6. AUSTRALIC

IMO 6503535 8,253g 8,100d.
149.21 o.l./137.16 b.p. x 18.90 x 9.36
metres.
Refrigerated capacity 367,670 cubic
feet.
2SCSA 8-cyl. Burmeister & Wain
874-VTBF-160-type oil engine by
Eriksbergs Mekaniska Verksted A/B,
Eriksberg, Sweden; 10,000 BHP, 19
knots.
12.10.1964: Launched by Eriksbergs
Mekaniska Verksted A/B, Eriksberg
(Yard No.594) for Rederiet for m.s.

'Australic' A/B, Gothenburg, Sweden
(Rederei A/B Transatlantic 50%,
Salenrederiana 50%) as AUSTRALIC.
23.3.1965: Delivered.
1978: Sold to Progress Compania
Naviera. S.A., Panama (Comninos
Brothers Shipping Co. S.A., Piraeus,
Greece) and renamed IONIAN
REEFER under the Greek flag.
1979: Owners now National Progress
Compania Naviera S.A., Panama
(Comninos Brothers Shipping Co. S.A.,
Piraeus).
1985: Transferred to Marine Heaven

S.A., Panama (Comninos Brothers
Shipping Co. S.A., Piraeus) and
renamed REEFER TIGER.
1985: Renamed REEFER TURBO.
1988: Managers now International
Maritime Transports Association S.A.,
Piraeus under the Greek flag.
1989: Transferred to Gemini
Maritime International S.A., Panama
(International Reefer Services S.A.,
Piraeus) under the Greek flag.
1992: Transferred to Maltese flag.
5.10.1993: Arrived Mumbai for
demolition by Rishi Ship Breakers.

Top: *Australic* in Salen colours.*[Russell Priest collection]*
Bottom: *Australic* as *Ionian Reefer* in Comninos funnel colours and rust. [*[FotoFlite incorporating Skyfotos 311277]*

PUTTING THE RECORD STRAIGHT

Letters, additions, amendments and photographs relating to features in any issues of 'Record' are welcomed (one letter below refers to issues number 17 and 18). Note that comments on multi-part articles are usually consolidated and included in the issue of 'Record' following the final part. Senders of e-mails are asked to provide their postal address. Letters may be lightly edited.

Allied War Coasters in the Mediterranean

John de S. Winter's article in 'Record' 52 was extremely interesting and informative. To complement it I can offer additional information on some losses.

The *Ardeola* and *Tadorna* (page 257) were intercepted by a Vichy warship and escorted into Bizerta on 9th November. The next day the Vichy Government placed its Tunisian bases at the disposal of the Axis. Both ships were taken over by Germany in early December, by which time *Tadorna* had been renamed *Balzac* by the French. On 7th March 1943 she was in a convoy from Tunis to Sicily which was attacked by six USAAF Mitchell bombers escorted by 14 Lightnings. The *Balzac* and the Italian *Ines Corrado* were sunk by bombs and another merchant ship damaged.

The *Ardeola* was handed to the Italians to manage and she was renamed *Aderno* by Societa 'Oriens', Trieste. On 23rd July 1943 she was torpedoed and sunk by HM Submarine *Torbay* whilst on passage from Naples to Civitavecchia.

The attack on shipping in Algiers Bay on 12th December 1942 was an example of the Italian Navy's ability to surprise the Allies by the use of unconventional weapons. Operation of these was concentrated in the 10th Light Flotilla. On the 4th December 1942 the specialist transport submarine *Ambra* (Lieutenant-Commander Mario Arillo) sailed from La Spezia for Algiers Harbour and Bay, where reconnaissance aircraft had identified large numbers of merchant ships. She carried three human torpedoes with their two-man crews and ten assault swimmers. The human torpedoes each carried two 150kg charges and the swimmers would each carry a sophisticated 4.5kg charge to be attached to ships' hulls. As well as a delay mechanism the charges had a propeller to delay activation until the ship was at sea.

At 21.45 on the evening of 11th the *Ambra* stopped on the seabed about two kilometres from the southern entrance to Algiers Harbour where six merchant ships were moored around her. The human torpedoes were launched with their operators and the ten frogmen. All had left for the target merchant ships by 23.20. The *Berto* was sunk by a human torpedo and other ships were damaged. The 16 Italians were not able to return to their submarine and all were captured. Vessels known to be damaged were *Ocean Vanquisher*, *Empire Centaur* and *Harmattan*.

Many ships were damaged and sunk by aircraft. The attacks on *Aurora*, *Tratanus*, *Speedfast*, *Dorset Coast*, *Uskside*, *Rossum*, *Nordeflinge* and *Devon Coast* were by German Junkers 88s.

The *Prins Willem III* and the *Saltwick* were torpedoed and sunk in attacks by German Heinkel He-111Hs of 1/Kampf Geschwader 26 with Junkers Ju-88As of 3/Kampf Geschwader 26.

The *Akabahra* was torpedoed and sunk in an attack by German Heinkel He-111Hs of 1/Kampf Geschwader 26.

The *Selbo* was torpedoed and sunk during an attack by Italian S.M.79s of 130 and 132 Gruppi.

The *Empire Kestrel* was torpedoed and sunk during an attack by Italian S.M.79s of 132 Gruppo.

The *Alpera* was bombed and sunk in the Bay of Biscay by a Focke-Wolf Fw-200 Kondor of Kampf Geschwader 40.
JOHN CHANDLER, Springwood, Little Kineton, Warwick CV35 0DP

British cargo ships and the 1940 Norwegian campaign (Part 2)

I think there is something amiss with the paragraph concerning *Pembroke Coast* ('Record' 57, page 44). *Dunluce Castle* was certainly not in Norwegian waters in May 1940. She had been withdrawn from service in June 1939 and sold for demolition, but reprieved and sent as a depot ship, initially to Immingham and, later in 1940, to Scapa. I doubt she was fit to go to sea. I assume the crew of *Pembroke Coast* were taken aboard HMS *Aurora* and shipped back to Scapa Flow where they might well have been accommodated aboard *Dunluce Castle*.
ALAN S. MALLETT, The Cabinet, High Street, Coltishall, Norfolk NR12 7AA

Selbo at Preston in 1938 or 1939. Built at Goole in 1921 for Norway as *Hubro*, she was renamed *Balder* for Swedish owners in 1932, returning to Norway as *Selbo* in 1938 for Einar Wahlstrøm, Oslo. She was torpedoed and sunk by Axis aircraft 15 miles from Cape Cavello, Algeria on 28th November 1942. *[World Ship Society Ltd.]*

Manganese and Messageries

No need to regret the price rise. The wonder is that you didn't do it long before and it certainly won't prevent my subscription renewal. Inflation has been low, of course, but compounding it over nearly eight years and recalling that giant leap in postage costs means that an extra pound is a very modest increase indeed.

I stand very properly corrected by Colin Menzies about that cargo out of Takoradi. The mineral berth there was only occasionally visited by liner companies since we were too busy loading timber and cocoa. Manganese to Newcastle was sometimes on offer in parcels of

The *Arbon* of 1954. *[FotoFlire incorporating SkyFotos/Roy Fenton collection]*

around two thousand tons which was of no interest to tramp traders. I'd completely forgotten about the bauxite exports. Smelting aluminium at the new port of Tema was one of the reasons for the Volta River hydro-electric project but I recall that the plant only enjoyed limited success.

The M.M. article was very interesting due to a very informative commentary by Dr. Burel. I especially enjoyed his honest account of the shortcomings of the *Euphrate* on page 20. The last Palm Line ships had an equally massive hatch opening, the twin hatch covers each measured 106 by 26 feet and were then the largest fitted to any British ship and aroused the keen interest of the Department of Trade and Industry. However, unlike the French vessel, the two derricks both reached the hold bottom and could work right up to the halfway point with ease. I mention this because the two vessels were of almost equal dimensions which just shows how naval architecture and derrick design had advanced between 1955 and 1982.

Finally, I can't leave this note without thanking John's Fylde collection for the photograph in this issue that might be telling a story. I refer to the picture of the *Rosaleen* at the foot of page 58. The single derrick attached to the foremast is supporting (via a hefty wire strop) the upper block of a very substantial three-fold purchase. So meaty, in fact, that one wonders if the derrick is man enough for it! Is it part of some manoeuvre to get her afloat again? Here's hoping that one of your reliably knowledgeable readers will also spot it and come up with an explanation.
JOHN GOBLE, 55 Shanklin Road, Southampton SO15 7RG

Great Yarmouth memories and mistakes

I was thrilled to read part 1 of your article about the Great Yarmouth Shipping Co. Ltd. Their ships were a large part of my life from the 1950s and 1960s when we were importing grain to Norwich. I was constantly on the phone to Small and Co. for information about our next grain cargo before we ran out of supplies for the mill. Many of the ships were Dutch coasters but the *Norwich Trader* was a regular visitor.

I have two photos of the *Norwich Trader*, one as she was swinging in the Turning Basin in Norwich and the second as she was proceeding downstream towards Carrow Bridge. This picture has the added interest that in the background is Henry Newhouse's ABC Wharf and between

the ship and the wharf is one of the company's lighters. Another of these craft is shown in the picture on page 194.

R.J. Read Ltd. owned the ABC Wharf at the time and we converted it into a grain store with a dryer and moved the grain to our mill about 400 yards downstream by lighter. The photos may not be of the quality to print as they are 35mm transferred to digital.

I always had a soft spot for the *Norwich Trader* (1), a lovely old steamer. I remember a day in the 1930s when she was stuck just below Norwich for several days due to low water - even though she only drew about eight feet. My father took me with him, and we went on board where they were transferring maize into a lighter to bring grain to the mill which was running out of supplies. I also vividly remember being allowed on the bridge of a coaster returning in ballast to Yarmouth, I think it was the *Lowestoft Trader* and the date was probably 1938.

You can understand the memories you have stirred. Keep up the good work.
BRYAN READ, 21 Upton Close, Norwich NR4 7PD

The middle photograph on page 2 is given as *Lynn Trader* which it is not. The photograph is repeated on page 9 and it says the ship became *Susan Olivier*. The text for M4 *Empire Farringdon* on page 9 also gives the name *Susan Olivier* but her name was actually *Susie Olivier* as can be seen from the photograph.
BOB TODD, Key Specialist Curator, Historic Photographs and Ships Plans Section, National Maritime Museum, London

'*Record*' 57 came thudding through my letterbox the other day and has provided its usual interesting mix of articles. The first one I read, being a coaster fan, was the second part of Great Yarmouth Shipping Company. However, I noticed that you've put in a little teaser to test your readers' powers of observation! As I'm sure a million people will have already fed back, the *Arbon* pictured on page 7 and the *Norfolk Trader* ex-*Arbon* pictured below it are not the same vessel. Although appearing similar at first glance, careful study reveals too many differences, including major ones such as the height of the poop, for them to be the same ship under different names.

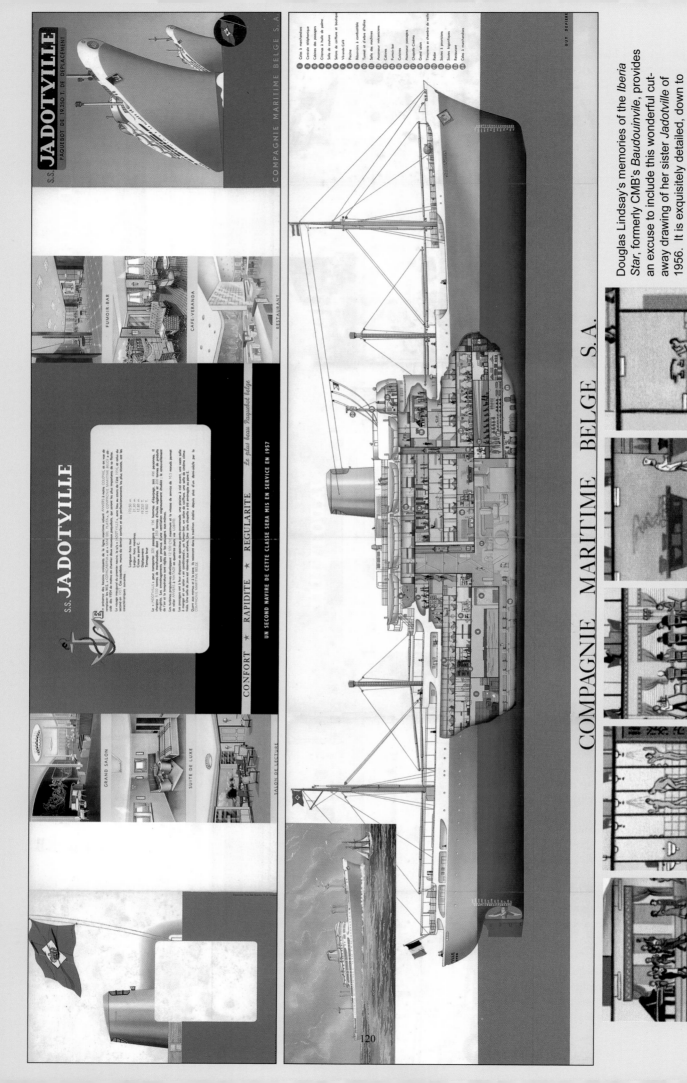

COMPAGNIE MARITIME BELGE S.A.

Douglas Lindsay's memories of the *Iberia Star*, formerly CMB's *Baudouinvile*, provides an excuse to include this wonderful cut-away drawing of her sister *Jadotville* of 1956. It is exquisitely detailed, down to showing figures dancing, showering, eating, cooking, or bathing (see the insets).

Although the reference material available to me is limited, consultation of my 1965 'Lloyd's Register' shows that there was at that time a Dutch coaster *Arbon* of 500 gross tons belonging to W.F. Kampman's Bevrachtingsbedrijf of Dordrecht. This ship was built in 1956 and I would guess that this is the *Arbon* shown in the photo.

Have I passed the test?
KEN LOWE, 4 Ansells, Seaview, Isle of Wight PO34 5JL
Thanks also to Paul Bertolo of Antwerp for spotting the difference between the photographs of Arbon *and the* Norfolk Trader. *It seems that, on selling the 1954-built* Arbon *to the Great Yarmouth company in 1956, her owners had ordered a slightly larger ship from her builders at Alphen an der Rhein which, as Ken Lowe points out, was completed the same year. Of 178.3 feet compared with 164.5 feet, the 1956* Arbon *had a more sharply raked bow and other detail differences. The accompanying photograph (page 119) shows the 1954-built* Arbon *which became* Norfolk Trader. *Apologies for errors. Ed.*

Memories of the *Iberia Star*

With my shiny brand new first mate's ticket in my pocket I went back to Blue Star Line and signed on as third mate of the *Iberia Star* (ex *Baudoinville*, 'Record' 55) on 6th March 1964. Newly transferred to Blue Star operation, she was commanded by Captain L. Vernon, Blue Star Line's commodore master and a war hero who had been captain of the *Brisbane Star* (11,076/1937) during the Malta convoy Operation Pedestal.

Joining *Iberia Star* was like stepping into a new world. She was spacious, comfortable and beautifully equipped. The cabins were all en suite, an unknown luxury to Blue Star officers – my previous ship, built for Blue Star later than *Iberia Star*, did not even have a wash hand basin in a cabin which would have fitted into my washroom on *Iberia Star*. The bridge was even more of a revelation – all mod cons, including a large modern radar set. The whole ship was on a different scale to anything I had known before and we were all delighted to be on her.

She fitted into the regular passenger run to South America, calling at Lisbon, Las Palmas, Rio de Janeiro, Santos, Montevideo, with turnaround at Buenos Aires. She was popular with passengers and we carried a good number on each trip. Although she did not have a large deadweight – my memory is of about 4,500 tons – she had a highly complex capacity from vegetable oil deep tanks through frozen and chilled meat lockers and dry cargo spaces to number one spar decks which had been adapted for carrying bananas.

So loading her was a complex process which could throw up its difficulties. I was mate of the deck while loading in Montevideo when we took in a parcel of frozen offal in small bags. These were bloodstained, torn and bashed and I 'claused' the mate's receipt accordingly. Next thing I am summoned to the captain's cabin where the shipper, the agents, the captain and various other high panjandrums were ranged in frosty silence – except for the shipper who was protesting at the top of his voice. Asked

to explain myself, I simply pointed out that that was the state they were in. This wasn't good enough – the shipper wanted clean bills which he could not have if the mate's receipt was 'claused'. So the chief officer was roused out of his bunk, much to his displeasure, and a delegation descended number two hold to inspect the offending items. They were indeed bloodstained, torn and bashed. I was dismissed with a flea in my ear and the assembly retired to the captain's cabin to argue the point. Eventually the whole consignment was landed ashore again and we were two hours late sailing, for which I was blamed for some obscure reason.

Life on board *Iberia Star* was very pleasant. The company, feeling greatly daring, had relaxed its rule banning ship's staff from having any contact with the passengers and for the first time ever on a Blue Star Line ship we were allowed into the upper deck veranda bar from five till seven in the evening, to mix with the passengers. Surprisingly, the ship did not immediately collapse into a drunken debauch and there was very little – if any – mischief in part I think because the passengers were very largely elderly couples. But the relaxation was watched closely with nervous anticipation.

Off the Casquets homeward bound each trip there were unpleasant experiences on the bridge. On the first trip, at two in the morning, we were groping our way along at dead slow in fog so dense we could not see the fore end of the ship even with the bridge so close. We picked up an echo on the radar, dead ahead and closing at 17 knots. It got closer and closer, we stopped and were sounding two long blasts but it kept coming and finally the echo merged with our centre spot. Braced for what seemed the inevitable collision we peered out into the murk. A very large Hapag Lloyd cargo ship passed down our starboard side no more than 20 feet away; how mutual suction did not drag us onto her I do not know, but she shot past and disappeared again as suddenly as she had come. Captain Vernon, who was a tough old bird, turned to me and said 'Well, I suppose you might as well give her dead slow ahead again'. But the German must have had an even bigger fright. A few minutes later we could hear him, out on our starboard quarter, sounding two long blasts.

The following trip I had the watch again in the same place but this time it was a bright sunny afternoon. The cross channel ferry *Caesarea* (4,174/1960) hove up at right angles

Caesarea at Weymouth on 1st June 1962. Completed at Cowes, Isle of Wight in 1960 for the British Transport Commission she served on the English Channel until 1980. After her sale to foreign buyers in 1980 renaming was simple - the C was deleted to give *Aesarea*. [J. and M. Clarkson]

on our port bow on a steady bearing. Captain Vernon was fond of playing bridge in the afternoons and I did not want to disturb him if possible. This wretched ferry got closer and closer without showing the slightest sign of altering course for us. At just over a mile away I put the ship into hand steering, sounded five short blasts, and started to swing hard to starboard intending to take a round turn out of us. But the blasts did their job – the ferry abruptly went hard to starboard, swung round under our stern missing by perhaps two ship's lengths. I quickly straightened us up again and resumed course. The blasts also brought Captain Vernon onto the bridge at the run. He looked around, saw the *Caesarea* tearing past us, proper precautions taken on our bridge, nodded and left again without ever saying a word. I got a good report that trip.
DOUGLAS LINDSAY, 3 Rectory Court, Old Banwell Road, Locking, Weston-super-Mare, North Somerset, BNS124 8BS

Fit for a king?

This is a long shot regarding the *Leopoldville* being dressed overall in the Mersey on 5th August 1934, photographs on pages 11 and 118 of 'Record' 54. Could it have something to do with the fact that King George V and Queen Mary had opened the (then) spectacular first Mersey Tunnel not long before this on 18 July?
DAVID ARIS, 1 The Stables, High Park, Oxenholme, Kendal, LA9 7RE

More on Talbot-Booth

Interested to read your article as I helped Talbot-Booth and David Greenman over the last 30 plus years, particularly with the accuracy of the drawings and the decision to go over to photographs. I agree with the content of your article, but as you observe there are quite a few gaps.

Talbot-Booth was at the 1937, 1953 and 1978 naval reviews as a commentator based on the *Patricia* in 1953 and the Royal Yacht in 1978. I was never clear when he actually retired from the Royal Navy but he was certainly associated with the Joint Forces Recognition Magazine (its office at Ashford closed about 2000). His collection contained many aerial shots with the office's stamp on the back. These photos, taken by RAF aircraft from various bases here and abroad, were sent to Talbot-Booth for identification. Many were of ships from the communist bloc.

Another point of interest was the publication of editions after 1940. Many copies fell into German hands either via their embassies in the USA or Argentina. Most German capital ships and commerce raiders had a copy. Belated security was the reason why new ships and war losses were not allowed for in the 1942 and 1943 editions.

I have seen a 1942 edition with a U.S. publisher's name on the title page but it retained the British advertisements.
TONY SMITH, 24 Balmoral Road, Kingsdown, Deal, Kent CT14 8DB

With reference to your query in 'Record' 57, I missed Volume 1, Number 1 of 'Ships', but I have the rest up to the final issue of Volume 4, Number 4.

Volume 1 ran from 10/1946 to 9/1947. Numbers 1 to 6 having a plain white cover with a drawing of ships in blue by Sargent. Numbers 7 to 12 had the same drawing but with a blue border.

Volume 2 ran from 10/1947 to 9/1948, with the same blue-bordered cover.

Volume 3 ran from 10/1948 to 9/1949, with an all-over blue on white dock scene on the cover.

Volume 4 ran from 10/1949 to 1/1950, with a photo of the launch of *Rangitane* on the cover, on a more glossy paper with a green border.

Talbot-Booth subsequently restarted with a magazine entitled 'Merchant Ships' which lasted for 20 months. Its format was more square than that of 'Ships'.
Volume 1 ran from 5/1954 to 4/1955
Volume 2 ran from 5/1955 to 12/1955.
FRED HAWKS, 25 Cherrytree Close, Billingshurst, West Sussex RH14 9NG

Talbot-Booth, Fowey and a faux pas

It was in 1959-60 when I regularly travelled from Liverpool to Douglas in the Isle of Man that I saw for the very first time ships I had only read about in the Ian Allan 'ABCs'. Buying a copy of the 1959 edition of Talbot-Booth opened up a completely new world for me. Now I could study the different designs of ships plus their layout and mast positions. In fact it taught me to be more observant when looking at vessels and I went as far as making crude sketches of some ships with special reference to their hull structure and mast layout.

I later acquired the 1963 and 1977-79 editions. That for 1963 was basically an update of 1959 and 1977-79 editions were disappointing. Gone were the different shadings in hull colour and funnel motifs. The drab grey drawings, although good, did little for me.

Having said this the 1977-79 did prove extremely useful in confirming the identity of ships seen when on holiday at Lovren, Jugoslavia in 1987. From our hotel balcony window I could easily see the ships arriving/sailing from Rijeka. Remembering the Talbot-Booth books I made sketches of the vessels seen and, on return to Falmouth with the aid of the books and more importantly 'Lloyd's List', I was able to identify a high percentage of the vessels seen.

The coloured drawings of the 1934 edition are most impressive although the black and white seem to lack a certain degree of authenticity. In the 1942 edition you become very much aware of how important and sizeable was the British merchant fleet. Photographs and fleet lists, plus the inclusion of major foreign companies, make this a real collector's album but who would have imagined at that time, that by the end of the century the British merchant fleet would be almost non-existent.

Good though the Talbot-Booth books were I still feel that the German drawings are superior. I still have the 1964 and 1968 editions of 'Deutschlands Handelsflotten' which include many drawings of the larger coasters plus the fleet lists of the major companies. The only fault of these books was that the reproductions were a little 'blotchy' in places. Since these editions other German books have perfected the art of reproduction so that the drawings are more clearly defined.

Sometimes a photograph raises more questions than it solves and so to 'Record' 56 – the bottom photograph on page 211. Here is a photograph of John Cory's tramps laid up at Fowey. Looking at this print I felt that the location was not correct. The hills in the background are too low for Fowey and the spit of land astern of *Ravenshoe* does not lend itself to Fowey. I am 99% certain that the vessels are laid up in the River Torridge between Bideford and Appledore which is confirmed by Norman Middlemiss in his book 'Travels of the Tramps', Volume 1.

'Record' 57 – bottom photograph on page 29. A good atmospheric photograph of local tug *Gallant* (see 'Record' 31) bound up river with Caffa Mill, the inlet which has since been filled in to form a car park, and the old railway line wending its way through the trees to Pinnock Tunnel. The latter is now used by road transport following the removal of all rail track.

'Record' 57 – top photograph on page 30. A real mystery photograph. *Cutty Sark* under tow with Polruan in the background. Has she just arrived from Falmouth as she is heading up river or is she being towed to a position off Pont Creek where she is to be turned? What is the name of the tug lying off her port quarter? Not *Gallant* as she had no lifeboat on her starboard side. Could it be a Falmouth tug – *New Resolute* is a possibility?
TERRY J. NELDER, 1 Sedgemead Court, Netley Abbey, Southampton SO31 5QB.
We are grateful for these and other readers who responded to our request in 'Record' 56 for more on Talbot-Booth and his books. For instance, Peter Hobday confirms that there was indeed an edition of 'Merchant Ships' in 1937, something the editors were only aware of from a bookseller's catalogue. Peter confirms that this contains coloured drawings of funnels and house flags as did the 1936 edition, and these have been expanded to eight pages for British Empire and 18 for other countries. These drawings were dropped for the 1939 edition. It seems that the listing in 'Record' 56 of the editions of 'Merchant Ships' was complete. Ed.

South West scenes and sins

The tug on page 29 of the latest edition of 'Record' is the Fowey-based *Gallant*, built by the Rother Ironworks at Rye in 1884 and which remained at Fowey under various owners until sold to W.J. Reynolds at Torpoint in 1954 and was not scrapped until 1963. She remains the longest-serving Fowey tug, operating at the port for 70 years. The barge she is towing is not strictly a lighter, but a dumb hopper barge owned by Fowey Harbour Commissioners and used to dump the spoil from dredging at sea.

STEPHEN CARTER, Clovenstones Cottage, Baldrine, Isle of Man IM4 6DS

PLM update

Whilst checking on a few details in the article about the PLM vessels in 'Record' 17 and 18, I came across some information that differs from that published. It comes from Uboat.net and Arnold Hague's database on Second World War convoys.

PLM 7 Torpedo fired by *U 442* failed to detonate. Sinking attributed to *U 522*.

PLM 12 Convoy was KS 65, Oran - Casablanca - Brest

PLM 19 Convoy was SL 78, Pepel – Middlesbrough.

PLM 27 Noted as seven crew members killed.
HOWARD (TED) NUTT, 17, Burnthill Crescent, Carnmoney, County Antrim, BT36 5AE.

Tees-made

Just a small correction for 'Record' 57, page 64. The trawler *Commandant Bultinck* was not 'another product of Smith's Dock at Stockton' as *Marloes* in 1911, but was of course from the South Bank yard which had been established in the previous year. Smith's Stockton yard was operational only in 1930-1931 and produced four freighters and nine trawlers, on the site occupied by Ropner between 1888 and 1925.
GEORGE ROBINSON, Southwood Cottage, Southwood Road, Cottingham, East Yorkshire HU16 5AJ

Antipodean photographers

On page 33 of 'Record' 57 the credit for the *Nanchang* photo was Doug Wright who passed away last year. In reading the request from William Burton on page 48 regarding the whereabouts of William Arthur Wilson's negatives, I recall that about 16 years ago I did an exhaustive search to record all the ship photographers in Australia and New Zealand but I never came across this chap, nor did any of the others mention him.
IAN J. FARQUHAR, RD2, Dunedin, New Zealand

We thought Terry may like to see a second picture of *Cutty Sark* at Fowey as this view shows the tug towing her. The inscription on the card is: 'Cutty Sark, Fowey harbour, August 1924'

According to 'Cutty Sark: Souvenir Guide' (a remarkably well researched, written and produced little booklet) she spent the years from 1922 to 1938 at Falmouth, leaving only once in 1924 to

be the flagship at the Fowey Regatta. Not surprisingly, local photographers recorded the visit of this celebrated ship.
[J. and M. Clarkson collection]

Photos from the Fylde - Record 57.

Long-term resident of Heysham, John Pryce has supplied further information and photos relating to some of the vessels referred to in the above article.

Wyresdale. Whilst laid-up at Glasson Dock she was bought by a Morecambe man, a Mr Bill Hogarth. He fitted her with a diesel engine, raised the bridge and used her on excursions from Morecambe harbour to the entrance to Heysham harbour, tides permitting. On other tides trips were made down the Grange Channel. The photo of her was taken off Heysham harbour entrance on Saturday, 12th August 1961. The trips continued for a number of years with *Wyresdale* retiring to Glasson each winter.

After Mr Hogarth passed away *Wyresdale* was abandoned at Morecambe where she was damaged by storm and fire. She became an eyesore there and was finally cut up for scrap by the local council on the Broadway Slipway where she is seen in the second and third photographs.

John adds it is interesting to note that in pre-war years *Wyresdale* ran trips from Fleetwood to battleships anchored out in Lune Deeps on courtesy visits. Passengers in those days were allowed on board the warships which included HMS *Emperor of India* in 1926, HMS *Malaya* in 1931 and HMS *Rodney* in 1936.

Atalanta. She was employed on the construction of the oil tanker jetty at Heysham early in the last war, arriving at Heysham in 1940 and leaving on 5th October 1941.

The Blackpool Steam Navigation Co. Ltd. was liquidated in 1947 and the Blackpool Steam Navigation Co. (1947) Ltd. was formed. It bought the Fairmile B motor-launch *ML 113* renaming her *Pendennis* and was their final ship. Initially she was registered at Liverpool but this was soon changed to Falmouth from where she operated until the 1950s when she returned to the north. *Pendennis* then operated from Blackpool Pier into Morecambe Bay on pleasure trips laying up at Glasson each winter and where she was finally broken up in the 1960s. When operating she would bunker at Heysham harbour and overnight there.

Wyvern. John and his brother Michael whilst still at school used to make trips on her, with the permission of her captain, James Hughes, when berthing tankers on the oil jetty. They were shown the saloon, below deck and aft of the accommodation, which was equipped with a bar but no longer in use by the 1950s. When completed in 1905 *Wyvern* had a passenger certificate for 232 but on 13th July 1931 her then captain, Joseph Benson, was caught with at least 325 people on board. This resulted in a fine of £5/0/0d and advocate fees of £2/2/0d. During the First World War, *Wyvern,* hired by the Admiralty in 1915, operated as a fleet tender at Scapa Flow with the name of *Wickstead* from July 1918 to October 1919 when she reverted to her own name. She also ran trips out to warships on courtesy visits anchored in Lune Deeps in the 1920s and 1930s.

Top: *Wyresdale* in Morecambe Bay after rebuilding and conversion from steam to diesel. Middle: Her derelict hulk on the beach at Morecambe where she was finally scrapped. *[John Pryce]* Bottom: *Pendennis* completing her refit at Glasson Dock and much later on the beach at Glasson in the 1960's where she was broken up. *[World Ship Society Ltd.]*

Electro identified

I am writing about the Gibraltar oil hulks correspondence in 'Record' 57 and in particular about the caption to the photograph of the *Norrisia*. The coaster alongside is the *Electro* owned by Ellerman's Wilson Line and managed by their subsidiary company the Antwerp Steamship Co. Ltd. The ship traded from the Irongate Wharf, adjacent to Tower Bridge, to Antwerp on a weekly basis from the late 1940s until 1967 when the service ceased. After the Irongate Wharf was sold to build the Thistle Hotel the trade carried on briefly from the Dundee Wharf in Limehouse. The service was twice weekly in conjunction with the General Steam Navigation Company who coincidentally owned the Irongate Wharf. Their regular ships included the *Cormorant* of 1927 which carried on until scrapped in 1957, the *Lapwing* of 1944, the *Sandpiper* of 1957 and the *Corncrake* of 1946.

Electro was completed in 1937 as *Williamstown* for the eponymous Williamstown Shipping Co. Ltd. (Comben Longstaff and Co. Ltd., managers) at N.V.Scheepswerf Gebroeders Van der Werf, Deest, Holland and was 793 gross tons and 447 net tons. She was powered initially by an MWM engine and re-engined with a British Polar in 1945. She was sold to Southampton owner William A. Wilson in 1940 and to Ellerman's Wilson Line in 1946.

My opinion about the photograph is that the *Electro* was taking a short 'rest' alongside the *Norissia* whilst awaiting the Esso bunkering berth at Purfleet when outward bound for Antwerp with some export cars on deck (Ford Anglias?). I believe that the tanker was not going anywhere as she seems securely moored fore and aft. The legend 'Jurgens' on the tall chimney indicates that the margarine factory of Jurgens and Van den Berghs, Purfleet, now a distant memory, was behind the *Norissia*.

Many thanks as ever for such a brilliant magazine.
BAYLY COLLYNS, 1 Hill Court, 8 Arterberry Road, London SW20 8AJ

Kaupo at Leith

I was delighted to see the photograph of the steamer *Kaupo* which was laid-up in Leith for quite a time (years, not months) in the latter part of the 1950s. I confirm that the photograph was taken in the Inner Harbour at Leith and that she is berthed on the east side of the Water of Leith (then still tidal as the large new lock at the northern end of the port had not yet been constructed). The photographer was standing at the entrance to the Old Docks on the west side of the Inner Harbour: they remained open (but were rarely used commercially) for a few more years and were subsequently filled in, the site now being occupied by

large office premises of the Scottish government. Astern of her was another long-term lay-up, the prototype freeze-at-sea trawler *Fairfree* owned by Christian Salvesen: memories can be unreliable after a period of almost 60 years but I'm pretty sure that her bow would have been visible in the photograph had she still been there. The *Fairfree* was towed away for scrap at the end of August 1957 so I'm reasonably confident that the photograph of the *Kaupo* was taken between then and her own removal under tow for scrapping just over two years later. I can also confirm from my surviving notes that the letter K on the white band on her black funnel was in green.

I'm very grateful to Charles Simpson, Graeme Somner and you for establishing that Cooper of Kirkwall had been part of the North Company. I'm therefore confident that the photograph of the *Amelia* in 'Record' 56 (which started this correspondence) was taken as she was waiting for the swing bridge to open for her to berth at the little wharf, just ahead of the *Kaupo*, which was used by the North Company until the late 1950s for its weekly cargo-only service between Leith and the Northern Isles, normally operated by their small motor ship *St Clement*. The other (larger) North Company ships used berths in the Outer Harbour.
COLIN MENZIES, 17 Bickenhall Mansions, London W1U 6BP

Electro. [J. and M. Clarkson collection]

Cormorant of 1927 in Thames on 8th June 1952. *[J. and M. Clarkson collection]*

Cormorant at Rock Ferry

Regarding the photo of *Cormorant* on page 128 of 'Record' 54 and the further piece on page 55 of 'Record' 57, I can categorically confirm that the photo is taken at the Rock Ferry slipway at the foot of Bedford Road, Rock Ferry. The elevated steel structure on the right of the photo is the 'Rock Ferry' ferry pier, which after closure of the ferry service on 30th June 1939 eventually became the Rock Ferry Tanker Cleaning Jetty - continuing in marine service until the early 1990s. Both structures still exist - the latter in a somewhat derelict condition - since the last operator, Veestore (a waste oil processor), pulled out.

I regularly used the Rock Ferry slip to launch my dinghy in order to row out to my own boat maintained on river moorings at Rock Ferry from the late 1970s to 2004. The slip (which is a public slipway) is still used today by the Royal Mersey Yacht Club and owners of other small craft moored at Tranmere and Rock Ferry.
NIGEL BOWKER, 9 Boulton Green Close, Spital, Bebington, Wirral L63 9FS

Probably taken during her long lay-up at Leith, this is Salvesen's fish factory trawler *Fairfree*. She had been built in Canada during 1944 as the minesweeper HMCS *Coppercliff*, later becoming HMS *Felicity*, and was bought by Fairfield Shipbuilding and Engineering Co. Ltd. in 1947 for conversion. Salvesen bought her in 1948, but by 1952 she was laid up, and remained so until sent to Charlestown, Fife in August 1957 to be broken up by Shipbreaking Industries Ltd. *[World Ship Society Ltd.]*

Digitisation of *Lloyd's List*

The British Newspaper Archive has now digitized in excess of six million pages of British newspapers to add to the two million provided by the British Library when the project started in the Autumn of 2011. A survey has been added to the BNA website to discover which newspapers people would like to see digitised next and an entry has been made for *Lloyd's List*. Readers who would like to support this idea can cast their own votes (up to three are allowed for any one paper or idea) by visiting the following website:
http://help-and-advice.britishnewspaperarchive.co.uk/forums/243704-newspapers-we-should-add-next
JOHN COOK by e-mail

RECORD REVIEW

ELLERMAN LINES: REMEMBERING A GREAT BRITISH SHIPPING COMPANY
Ian Collard
Softback 23.3 x 15.5 cms of 236 pages
Published by The History Press, Stroud at £16.99.

The Ellerman group was a very significant entity. Sir John Ellerman built up one of the largest British shipping conglomerates, its large fleet operating services to Scandinavia, the Baltic, the Mediterranean, South and East Africa, and the Indian subcontinent, with extensions to North America and Australasia. The founder's determination to impose a corporate identity in terms of names, hull and funnel colours across its entire fleet (except for Ellerman's Wilson Line) gave its ships a distinct identity unmatched by those of any other major British shipping group.

Highly successful in its day, the Ellerman group merits a detailed history which examines its business strategy, finance, construction policy and philosophy as well

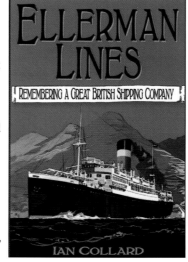

as its fleet. This it has yet to receive. It has previously had 'Ellermans: A Wealth of Shipping' by one-time deputy chairman James Taylor which provides a corporate view of its rise. It also has the 1989-published 'Ellerman Lines', number 10 in Duncan Haws' 'Merchant Fleets' series, which offers a somewhat breathless chronology, accompanied by details and careers of each ship, all illustrated by profile drawings. Serious researchers regard Duncan Haws' books as offering a first draft of a company's history, and those who look at them closely often find numerous minor, but annoying, errors. However, they are well-meaning attempts to chronicle important fleets, and represent a great deal of first-hand research.

'Ellerman Lines: Remembering a Great British Shipping Company' begins with a narrative history that parallels Duncan's chronology, and continues with a detailed list of ships owned by each of the group companies, omitting Ellerman's Wilson Line (as did Haws). The fleet list is even closer to that in Haws' book, repeating some of its mistakes, with some additional data for certain later ships which appears to have come from contemporary trade publications. Given the sources listed, little original research can have taken place, and the book appears to be largely an exercise in typing.

Black and white photographs, plus some advertisements, are reproduced at points in the text; these are clearly reproduced but in many cases only to the size of cigarette cards. The History Press, in common with other publishers based near Stroud, is notorious for failing to credit photographs, and neither publishers nor author appear to have sought permission from negative holders to use the images chosen.

Ian Collard's book offers little more than a reworking of Duncan Haws' book and, although this author is listed in the acknowledgements, it is not made clear whether permission has been given to use his work. If so, one assumes known errors would have been corrected. Both the fleet list and history have been brought up to date, but in several respects Haws' work is superior, in that every class of

ship is illustrated by line drawings, and the ships are indexed according to their Ellerman names.

The complete lack of an index in the new book seriously reduces its usefulness. The ships are listed in chronological order of their acquisition, with separate lists for each individual company in the Ellerman group. Hence in order to find a particular entry the user needs to know not only which of at least six companies owned the ship but also its date of acquisition: this reviewer soon gave up trying. Indexing is tedious work, but it would have made this book useable.

Searching for something positive to say, 'Ellerman Lines' is at least economically priced, it offers the only history and fleet list of the Ellerman group currently in print, and the colour reproduction of a poster on the cover is attractive. However, in most other respects it is a retrograde step, and a major opportunity to properly chronicle an important fleet has been wasted. The Ellerman group, and those interested in it, deserve better.

Roy Fenton

BOSUN'S LOCKER

57/01 and 57/02 *Umvolosi*

Not only have we had confirmation of the position where *Umvolosi* went ashore, but also a date for the incident and a brief biography of her master. David Hodge, Bert Spaldin and Alan Mallett concur that she ran aground on 13th April 1907 in the Hartlepool entrance channel at about 6.00am whilst entering the port to load for South Africa. A strong south easterly wind probably caught her as she turned to port at the dog leg in the channel, which is only a few ship's length astern of her. Bert points out that ships could get to West Hartlepool this way, but that the port did have its own entrance just to the south of Hartlepool.

Alan tells us that her master was Captain C. Hedley (1870-1932) who from 1901 commanded seven of Bullard, King's ships. These included the *Umbilo* (1,923/1890) which was wrecked on 26th May 1903, when he is recorded as 'acting creditably'. Neither does the *Umvolosi* grounding seem to have harmed the captain's career, as he was immediately appointed to the command of *Umtali* (2,641/1896).

57/03

This photograph, on page 10, still waits positive identification. Suggestions have been made that she might be one of the big Glen Line steamers built from 1913 onwards, but the mast arrangements do not match. The fire damage apparent (and complete lack of boats) led to a suggestion from Vic Pitcher that she might be Blue Funnel's *Menestheus* of 1929 after catching fire off the coast of California in April 1953. *Menestheus* would, one presumes, have been rebuilt after her war service as a floating brewery, but 57/03 looks nothing like her pre-war or wartime appearance. Tore Nilsen found a near-match in the 1959 Talbot-Booth, where the drawing numbered 409 shows the Soviet-owned *Minsk*. This steamer was built in 1918 in Germany as *Forst* and surrendered to the U.K. in 1919 to become Hogarth's *Baron Ogilvy*. Subsequent names were *Murla* under the German flag, and *Minsk* from 1932. This looks like a very near miss,

as the photograph of *Murla* on page 41 of Arnold Kludas' book on Norddeutscher Lloyd shows a similar ship but with a number of significant differences, lacking the kingposts at the after end of the accommodation block and having no poop structure. However, the similarities strongly suggest that 57/03 shows a German-built ship dating from around the time of the First World War. Further suggestions are welcome.

The Bosun boobs

In the photograph on page 56 of the end of an Elder Dempster ship in the Elbe, only the first letter of her name is visible. The Bosun remembered it as the *Oti*, although it was actually the *Ondo*. Thanks to Michael Cranfield, David Hodge and Alan Dean who pointed out the error, the latter sending much supporting material. The *Ondo* and her grounding was covered in 'Record' 45.

Nikobar and *Abergeldie*

The Bosun recently acquired the accompanying photograph of the *Nikobar*, built at Copenhagen for the Danish East India Company in 1906 (opposite page, top). Written on it is 'Abergeldie and Nikobar - Salvage award £8,000, 21st January 1908'. The starting point for research was Ole Stig Johannesen's 'The EAC Fleet', which notes that, during the homeward leg of her first round voyage to the Far East, a serious fire broke out on *Nikobar* whilst in the Gulf of Aden. No further information is given, and it can only be assumed that the Aberdeen-registered steamer *Abergeldie* (3,777/1898) came to her rescue, meriting a generous if belated salvage award. The almost new *Nikobar* (which at 3,453gt was larger than she looks in this photograph) was repaired and in August 1907 passed to Swedish owners, being broken up as *Carlsholm* in 1934. The accompanying photograph, on the Scheldt, was probably taken just before she set out on her ill-fated maiden voyage. Any further information on the 1906 incident would be welcome.

58/1. What looks like a railway steamer (right) but which one and what has happened to her - war damage or the result of an accident? The only clue to the origin of the photograph is the Calais postmark.

58/2. A large photograph picked up at a recent sale (below). Can anyone throw any light on this picture, the name of the ship hopefully and details of her plight? There is no indication on the picture as to when or where it was taken however the barge has the name S E Snow, Nome on its side. The ship's name appears to be made up of at least five letters and the port of registry seven. She has a five pointed star on her funnel.